SIMLA VILLAGE TALES

OR, FOLK TALES FROM THE HIMALAYAS

SIMLA VILLAGE TALES

OR, FOLK TALES FROM THE HIMALAYAS

ALICE ELIZABETH DRACOTT

GYAN

Published by

GYAN

Gyan Publishing House
5, Ansari Road
Daryaganj, New Delhi-110002
Phone: 011-47034999, 9811692060
E-mail: books@gyanbooks.com

Distribution Network
gyanbooks.com
India, USA, Canada, UK, Australia

ISBN: 978-93-7169-457-5 (PB)

First Published, 1906

2nd Impression 2025

Printed at: Gyan Press, Delhi.

**SIMLA VILLAGE TALES:
OR, FOLK TALES FROM THE HIMALAYAS**
Author: ALICE ELIZABETH DRACOTT

A Simla Village Woman
From a Snapshot by A. E. D.

[*Frontispiece.*

SIMLA VILLAGE TALES

OR, FOLK TALES FROM THE HIMALAYAS

BY ALICE ELIZABETH DRACOTT

LONDON

JOHN MURRAY, ALBEMARLE STREET, W.

1906

TO THE ONE I LOVE BEST.

PREFACE

In introducing "Simla Village Tales" to my readers, I wish to acknowledge gratefully the valuable assistance given me by my sister Mabel Baldwin, who, when I was obliged to leave India suddenly owing to nervous break-down after the terrible earthquake which visited the Punjaub in April 1905, kindly undertook to complete, from the same sources where I had got them, my collection of folk-tales. Twenty excellent stories contributed by her include "Tabaristan," "The Priest and the Barber," "The Fourth Wife is Wisest," and "Abul Hussain."

Of the down-country tales my husband kindly contributed "Anar Pari," "The Dog Temple," "The Beautiful Milkmaid," and "The Enchanted Bird, Music, and Stream." Both my sister and my husband can speak the language fluently, and as the former has resided many years in the Punjaub, I am confident that her translations are as literal as my own. All the tales were taken down in pencil, just as they were told, and as nearly as possible in the words of the narrators, who were village women belonging to the agricultural class of Hindus in the Simla district.

I must add a word of thanks to Mr Hallam Murray for his invaluable assistance with the illustrations.

In one or two instances I was asked if I would allow a Paharee man, well versed in local folk-lore, to relate a few stories to me; but, for obvious reasons, I was obliged to decline the offer, for many Simla Village tales related to me by women, and *not* included in this book, were grotesquely unfit for publication.

The typical Paharee woman is, as a rule, extremely good-looking, and a born flirt; she has a pleasant, gay manner, and can always see a joke; people who wish to chaff her discover an adept at repartee.

The "Simla Village Woman," whose photograph is reproduced, is a very good type. I found her most gentle and lovable. Her little boy, and last surviving child, has died since the photograph was taken last year, yet the young mother bears all her griefs with a fortitude which is really remarkable.

Himalayan folk-lore, with its beauty, wit, and mysticism, is a most fascinating study, and makes one grieve to think that the day is fast approaching when the honest rugged hill-folk of Northern India will lose their fire-side tales under the influence of modern civilisation.

The hurry and rush of official life in India's Summer Capital leaves no time for the song of birds or scent of flowers; these, like the ancient and exquisite fireside tales of its people, have been hustled away into distant valleys and remote villages, where, on cold winter nights, Paharees, young and old, gather together to hear these oft-repeated tales.

From their cradle under the shade of

ancient deodars, beside the rocks, forests and streams of the mighty Himalayan mountains, have I sought these tales to place them upon the great Bookshelf of the World.

A. E. D.

CONTENTS

THE CAUSE OF A LAWSUIT BETWEEN THE OWL AND THE KITE

THE owl and the kite once went to law on these grounds. The owl said that she was the oldest creature in the world, and that when the world was first made, she alone existed. The kite objected. He said that he flew in the air and lived in the trees.

To prove which was right they went to law, and the owl pleaded that, since there were no trees at the beginning of the world, the kite was wrong in saying that he had lived in trees. The Judge therefore decided in favour of the owl.

A MONKEY OBJECTS TO CRITICISM

A MONKEY once sat on a tree, shivering with cold, as rain was falling, and a little bird sat in its nest on the same tree; and, as it sat, it looked at the monkey and wondered why a creature with hands and feet like a man should shiver in the cold, while a small bird rested in comfort.

At last it expressed its thought to the monkey, who replied: "I have not strength to build myself a house, but I have strength to destroy yours," and with that he pulled to pieces the poor little bird's nest, and turned it out with its young.

THE DEAD MAN'S RING

A YOUNG married woman one night listened to the jackals' cry, and heard them say: "Near the river lies a dead man; go and look on his finger and you will find a ring worth nine lakhs of rupees." She therefore rose and went to the riverside, not knowing that her husband secretly followed in her footsteps. Arrived there, she found the dead man, but the ring was difficult to remove, so she drew it off with her teeth.

Her husband, who did not know she had understood and acted upon the cry of the jackals, was horrified, and thought she was eating the flesh of the dead man; so he returned home, and when the morning came, took his wife to her mother, and said: "I have brought back your daughter, and refuse to live with her any longer, lest I come to some evil end." He gave no reason for having thus said, and returned to his home.

In the evening his wife sat sorrowfully in the

garden of her father's house, and the crows came to roost in the peepul trees; and as they came, they said: "In this place are buried four boxes containing hidden treasure: dig and find it, O my daughter." The young girl called her parents and told them the message of the crows. At first they laughed, but, after a while, they dug as she directed, and found treasure which enriched the whole family. The girl then explained the story of the dead man's ring, and her husband gladly forgave her and received her back.

THE ORIGIN OF DEATH

WHEN God first made the world, He took two handsful of ashes and placed them in a corner and hid Himself. These became a man and a woman. God then called the man by name, saying: "Manoo," and the man replied, "Hoo" instead of "Ha Jee" (Yes Life) respectfully, as he should have done.

For this reason was everlasting life denied him, and where he stood, there were his ashes when he died. Even to this day, if a man should scratch himself, a line of white ash of which he was made is seen. If any man addresses another as "Jee" it is accounted to his good.

THE REAL MOTHER

THERE was once a Rajah who had seven wives; six of these were rich and dwelt in his Palace, but the seventh was poor, and lived apart in a little mud hut by herself. The Rajah had one great sorrow, and that was that he had no children. One day he went out to *shikar* (or hunt) and saw an old Fakir lying fast asleep. He did not know that the Fakir had been asleep for twelve years; so he pressed his hands and feet, and the old man awoke. Seeing the Rajah sitting beside him, he thought he had been attending him for twelve years, so he said: "What is your wish, my son?" and the Rajah said: "I have no children. I want neither riches nor honour, but a son." Then the old Fakir gave him his staff, and said: "Go to yonder mango tree and hit it twice, bring away any fruit which may fall to me."

The first time the Rajah hit the tree only six mangoes fell, and the next time only one;

these he carefully carried to the old Fakir, who told him to take them home, and give one each to the Ranees, and they would each have a son.

So the Rajah returned to his Palace, and gave them to his six Ranees, but quite forgot the poor Ranee, who lived apart by herself. The six Ranees did not believe what the old man said, so they just tasted the fruit and then threw it away; but when the poor Ranee heard what had happened, she told her servant to go and look in the drain for any mangoes the others had thrown away, and bring them to her; so the servant brought them, and she carefully ate every one. Three months afterwards she sent for an old nurse, or dhai, who told her that she would soon be a mother.

The Rajah was passing by when he saw the old nurse coming out of the poor Ranee's hut, so he made enquiries; and, when he heard the news, there were great rejoicings in the Palace. This made the other six Ranees very angry indeed, and they called the old dhai and told her that if, when the child was born, she would promise to kill it, they would give her a great reward. When the day came the wicked old dhai who was in attendance on the Ranee, said: "Ranee, I must blindfold your eyes." The Ranee consented, and while thus blindfolded, became the mother of six sons and one daughter.

As soon as they were born, the old dhai carried them outside and threw them into a hole in a potter's field, and there left them to die, while she told the Ranee that she had given birth to a piece of iron! The poor Ranee was terribly disappointed, and so was the Rajah, but they submitted to what they thought was the will of God. But the potter's wife found the children, and as she was childless, she carried them home and looked well after them, so that they all lived and grew.

This came to the ears of the six Ranees, and they called the old dhai, and said: "What is this we hear? you did not kill the children; they are alive and living in the house of the potter, but if you listen to us and go and kill them, we shall give you all the jewels that we possess." So the wicked old woman made some sweet chappatis, or hand cakes, and carried them to the well where the children used to play every day. She found them there playing with their toy horse and toy parrot, cheap toys made of clay by their foster-father, the potter, and they were soon tempted to eat her sweets. No sooner had they done this, when all seven fell down and died.

The poor potter and his wife found them thus when they came to search for them some hours later; and, although the woman wept, the man at once set out in search of the old Fakir, and as soon as he found him he told him what had happened. The old Fakir cut his finger and drew some blood: this he gave to the potter, and said: "Go quickly and sprinkle this on the children, and they will live."

The potter did as he was told, and the children came to life again, and went to live with their foster-parents as before. This also came to the ears of the six cruel Ranees, and they again called the old dhai and told her she must make another attempt to kill the children.

This time she had some difficulty in persuading them to eat her sweets, for they remembered what had happened before; but in the end she succeeded, and left them all lying dead on the ground as before.

The poor potter was quite broken-hearted, and again sought help of the old Fakir. The old Fakir said: "Son, I cannot raise the children to life in the same way a second time, but bring them here to me."

So he brought them, and the Fakir said: "Dig seven graves, and in the centre an eighth grave for me, and bury us all." This the potter did, and lo! after a time a mango tree sprang from the grave of each brother, a beautiful rose from the grave of the sister, and a chumpa or very sweet-flowering tree from the grave of the old Fakir.

One day the servants of the Rajah saw these trees, and, being struck with the beauty of the roses, went to gather some; but as they stretched out their hands to do so, the bough raised itself beyond their reach and said: "Brothers, may I let them gather roses?" And the brothers replied: "Ask the old Fakir." So they asked him, and he said: "None but thy mother may gather roses of thee."

Much impressed by what had happened, the Rajah's servants went and told him all they had heard and seen, and forthwith he set out to see the trees. He too tried to gather flowers, but found he could not do so.

Then he remembered the old Fakir and the seven mangoes, and sent at once for his six Ranees, to see if any of them could gather the strange roses. Each tried in turn, and the tree said as before: "Brothers, may I give roses to my mother?" The brothers replied: "Ask the old Fakir;" but the answer was always the same: "These are not to gather roses, they are for thy mother alone."

On this the Rajah sent for the poor, neglected Ranee, who, as we know, was the real mother; and as soon as she came, the rose branches spread themselves low on the ground, and she was soon covered with beautiful flowers.

When this happened the old Fakir's grave opened, and he came back to life, and brought the brothers and sisters with him. He told the whole story of the six Ranees' cruelty, and the old dhai's wickedness to the Rajah, who forthwith ordered them all to be killed, and lived happily ever after in his Palace, with his seven children, and their mother, the once poor, neglected Ranee.

THE PRINCESS SOORTHE

Two sisters, the daughters of a Rajah, were betrothed to two Princes, the eldest to a poor man with few followers, the youngest to a rich man with many followers. About eight days before their marriage, the elder called the younger and said: "Sister, we shall not be long together, let me comb your hair for you beside the well;" but in her heart she was jealous of her sister Soorthe, and had it in her mind to kill her, for she did not wish her to marry a rich man.

Now in the well were some frogs, so the elder sister said: "Sister, do you see these frogs? The name of the Rajah you are about to marry is Dhuddoo, or Frog, and you think that he is a man, but he is, in reality, a frog."

This so alarmed Soorthe that she wrote at once to the Rajah to say she would not marry him, and he replied that he accepted her letter and would marry elsewhere; but he was vexed at the letter, and took good care to come in a grand procession which passed beneath the windows of the Princess.

She did not know it was her former lover passing by, and asked which man in the procession was the Rajah; thus was it explained to her who he really was, and how her elder sister had deceived her, and as she caught sight of him she foolishly thought he had come back for her; so she let herself down with ropes from her window: but only to fall into the hands of some thieves, who took her away, and left her in the forest, where she was found by a Dhobie, or washerman, who sold her to a dancing girl.

This woman taught Soorthe to dance; and, hearing that a Rajah in the vicinity was entertaining a guest, and giving a feast and a nautch, the two set out. This Rajah was entertaining Soorthe's father, although she did not know of it, and when he recognised his own daughter, who had been brought up in strict purdah, dancing in public, like a common dancing girl, his wrath knew no bounds.

He ordered her nose to be cut off forthwith, and had her turned out of the kingdom. Thus do the innocent sometimes fall victims to the deceit of others, and thus do they follow in the footsteps of evil associates.

THE SNAKE'S BRIDE

THERE was once a Rajah, by name Bunsi Lall, who was charmed by a witch, turned into a snake, and lived under ground, but he constantly wished to go above ground and see the world.

So one day he ran away and made himself a house above ground. Now, at this time there was a girl living in that place who had a very cruel stepmother, and this woman made her spend the whole day picking up sticks in the forest. It was there the snake met her, and was struck with her beauty, and one day he said to her: "Sukkia, child of Dukhia (or the one who gives you pain), will you marry me?" But the girl was afraid, for who would marry a snake?

She did not know that the snake was Rajah Bunsi Lall, and that he was only a snake by day, but resumed his human form at night, so she went and told her stepmother all about it; and her stepmother, who did not care what became of the girl, said: "Tell him you will marry him if he fills your house with silver." This the girl told him, and he readily agreed.

Next day, when her stepmother opened the door, she found her house filled with silver, and readily gave her consent to the marriage; so Sukkia became the snake's bride, and went to live in his house, where all was comfort and happiness for her.

After some time her stepmother thought she would go and find out whether the girl was still living; and when she arrived at the snake's house, she found that, contrary to her expectations, Sukkia was both happy and prosperous.

Now the stepmother knew the story of the enchantment of Rajah Bunsi Lall, and also that, if he revealed his name, he would be obliged to return again to his former home under ground; and she advised Sukkia to beg him to tell his name, and not to rest day or night until he had done so.

When night came, Sukkia asked her husband to tell her his name; but he

THE SNAKE'S BRIDE

"Sukkia, child of Dukhia, will you marry me?"

[*To face page* 16.

implored her not to, as it would bring bad luck to her, yet she persisted in asking, and would not be advised, though he turned himself into a snake and fled before her till he reached the river-side, where he again begged her to desist; but the foolish girl would not listen, till he called out: "My name is Rajah Bunsi Lall;" and so saying he disappeared under the water, and she saw him no more.

For days and days she wandered the streets and bazaars calling, "Rajah Bunsi Lall, Rajah Bunsi Lall!" but he came not, and she was very unhappy. In the meantime the snake had reached his own country, where arrangements were being made to marry him to another girl; and when his servants came to draw water from the well, they met Sukkia and told her of it.

Now Sukkia still wore the ring which Rajah Bunsi Lall had given her, and she begged them to take it to him, which they did; and when his eyes fell upon it he remembered Sukkia, and all she must have suffered because of him, so he went back to the world determined to seek and find her, and then bring her to his own country. Sukkia was delighted to meet him again. and gladly followed him; but the snake's mother soon discovered her, and made up her mind to kill her without delay, so she had a room prepared full of scorpions and snakes, and all sorts of deadly creeping things, and invited Sukkia to sleep there.

This plot was discovered in time by Rajah Bunsi Lall; and he had the creatures all removed and the room swept clean and whitewashed, thus Sukkia escaped; but only for a time, for the snake's mother told her she was clever, indeed so clever that a test would be given her to prove her cleverness, and if she failed to give proof of it, she would be put to death.

The snake's mother then brought a quantity of mustard seed and strewed it on the floor beside Sukkia, telling her to divide it into equal lots and carefully count each seed.

The poor girl began to cry, for she felt this task to be beyond her power, and the snake said all the trouble had been caused through asking his name, but he knew some little birds, who came when he called them by name, and they very soon divided the mustard seed, so once again Sukkia escaped.

The next time she went out, it was to follow very miserably in the wedding procession of the snake; and his mother had arranged that Sukkia should have torches to carry on her head and in her two hands, so that, when the wind blew towards her, she would be burnt to death. All happened as arranged, but when Sukkia cried out, "I am burning, I am burning!" Rajah Bunsi Lall heard her and quickly ran to her rescue. Together they ran away and escaped to the upper world, and found their former home, where they lived happily ever after.

THE POWER OF FATE

THERE was once a Rajah who had six daughters, none of whom were married, although all were grown up.

One day he called them to him, and asked each in turn whether she was satisfied with her lot in life and what fate had given to her. Five of the daughters replied: "Father, our fate is in your hands: you feed and clothe us, and all that is to be provided for our future you will provide: we are well satisfied with our lot in life." The youngest daughter alone kept silent, and this vexed her father, who enquired why she made no reply.

"My fate is in no one's hands," she said; "and whatever is to be, will be, whether so willed by my father or not."

The Rajah was now angrier than before, and ordered that she should be immediately put to death; but upon second thoughts he decided to send her to a distant forest, and there leave her without food or water, so that she might

The Power of Fate

Took out the fan and began to wave it.

[*To face page* 20.

either be eaten by wild beasts at night, or else die of starvation.

So she was placed in a dooly or litter and carried away. The dooly-bearers took her to a very dense jungle, and at length arrived at a clear space, in the centre of which stood a huge oak tree. Here they determined to leave her, so they tied the dooly to the boughs of the tree, where it could swing above ground, and departed.

Now the Princess was very religious, so she spent her time in reading, and said her prayers five times a day, believing that if it were her fate to die she would die, but if not, some help would be sent to her.

In this way day after day passed by without any relief, and the poor Princess was both hungry and cold, yet she continued to pray each day, until, on the morning of the ninth day, Mahadeo (or God), who had heard her unceasing prayers, called one of his messengers and said: "Some one on the earth is in great pain and sorrow, and her prayers are ever knocking at my door; go thou to seek who it is, and bring me word."

So the messenger went forth, and found the poor Princess in her dooly on the tree, so he quickly brought back the news to Mahadeo, who sent him back with food and water to her relief.

After she had eaten and drunk, she washed the brass vessels in which her food had come, and continued to pray and give thanks to God. Now each day fresh food and water was sent to her, and for her faith and goodness, Mahadeo determined to give her a reward.

Looking out of her dooly one day, she noticed that the earth looked wet in a certain spot, so she dug there with her nails, and found water; not only did she find water, but stones, which were all of solid gold and silver. "My fate has indeed been good," said the Princess, and she forthwith determined to build herself a Palace on that spot, and to surround it with a beautiful garden.

Next day she heard a woodman felling trees in the forest, and called loudly to him. The man was afraid, for it was a lonesome spot, where he had never before heard the sound of a human voice, and he thought she must be a spirit; but the Princess assured him that she too was human, and a King's daughter, who had been banished, and promised that if he would only bring her wood to build with, and workmen to make her house, she would pay him in gold daily.

Pleased at his luck, the woodman lost no time in calling carpenters and masons, and before long a lovely Palace and garden were made in the once jungly spot, and here the Princess with her servants lived a very happy life together.

One day the King, her father, riding by that way, was greatly surprised when he saw what a beautiful house and garden had been made in the midst of the jungle. He sent his servants to enquire whose it was, and to bring word quickly concerning it.

The Princess saw her father's servants, and ordered that they should be kindly treated, and fed on the best of food; so they returned well pleased, to tell the King that it was his long-lost daughter, whom he had thought was dead, that owned the Palace, and she had sent a message to ask him to come and see her.

The Rajah was indeed surprised, and hastened to find out for himself whether or not the news were true. When the Princess met him she reminded him of what she had said about fate, and her belief that what was to be, would be in spite of all efforts to prevent it, so that the Rajah also was convinced that she was right.

After this her sisters came to visit her, and she gave them many beautiful and costly presents. Not long afterwards the Rajah made up his mind to travel, and asked each of his five children what they would like him to bring her on his return. They all wanted something different, and he had almost forgotten to ask his youngest daughter what she wanted, as she already had all that heart could wish, but he felt ashamed to leave her out, so he asked her also.

"I have all that I need, O my father, but if, in your travels, you come to a certain city where there is a little box for sale, bring it to me."

The Rajah soon bought his five daughters their presents, all but the little box, so when he arrived at the city his youngest daughter had mentioned, he began to enquire if there was a little box for sale.

Now it was well known in that place that a certain bunniah had in his safe keeping a magic box which contained a fan, and the soul of a king's son. If any one waved the fan forwards, the Prince would at once appear, but waved backwards he would at once disappear.

When the people heard a Rajah asking for a box, they thought that it was this magic box he meant, so they directed him to the bunniah, who said he might have it for five hundred rupees. This seemed a large sum to pay for so small, and, as it appeared to him, common a thing, yet, rather than return without it, the Rajah paid the price and returned to his own country. His five daughters were delighted with their gifts, and he sent the box to the youngest Princess.

She soon opened it, took out the fan, and began to wave it. No sooner had she done so when a fine handsome Prince stood in her presence; but, when she waved in the opposite direction from herself, he disappeared.

Every morning the Princess summoned the Prince with her fan, and during the day they spent many pleasant hours together playing Pacheesee, or Oriental Chess: in the evening she sent him away. The two were always happy together, and never weary of each other's presence, which, I am told, is a sign of the truest friendship.

The five sisters soon came to show their youngest sister their presents; and laughed when they saw a simple little box, asking what made her choose such a plain common thing.

Upon this the foolish girl told them the whole secret of the box, and taking out the magic fan, waved it in their presence, and the Prince arrived as before.

This made the five elder sisters very angry and jealous; and while they sat together playing chess, they planned mischief in their hearts; so that evening they got some glass, and pounded it into little bits, and this they spread upon the couch on which the Prince was wont to take his midday rest. Next day, when he came, the bits of glass hurt the poor Prince cruelly; but, being a guest, he made no remark, and in the evening departed to his home, where, before long, he became very ill indeed.

The King, his father, summoned all the cleverest Hakeems, or native physicians, to his son's bedside; but they could do nothing, and day by day the poor Prince lay at the point of death. In vain the Princess waved her fan; he was too ill to respond, and the five cruel sisters rejoiced to think their plan had succeeded so well.

At last the youngest Princess could bear her suspense no longer; so, calling her servants together, she told them she was going by herself to a distant country on a pilgrimage, dressed like a Fakir, and none must follow her.

At first her servants would not consent, and declared they would follow wherever she went, but after a time the Princess had her way, and set out on her journey.

She wandered many miles that day, and at evening, weary and footsore, sat down under a tree to rest. While she sat there an eagle and a parrot began to talk in a neighbouring branch. "What news?" began the parrot.

"Have you not heard of the magic box, and the Princess, and how her sisters placed broken glass on the couch of the Prince, and how even now he lies at the point of death?"

"This is indeed sad news; and is there no remedy for his illness?"

"The remedy is simple, if they but knew it. You have only to gather the refuse from an eagle's nest, add water to it, and apply it to the hurt, when, after three applications, the glass will come away, and the flesh speedily heal."

This conversation was eagerly listened to by

the Princess; and afterwards she carefully gathered the refuse beside the eagle's nest, and again started with all haste on her journey.

Arrived at the town, she began to cry in the streets, "A Hakeem, a Hakeem!" (or doctor), and was instantly summoned to the King's Palace; for he had promised even to give up his kingdom to any one who would save his son. So the Princess in this disguise hastened into the King's presence, and there arranged to treat the Prince, on condition that no other remedy should be tried by others at the same time.

At the first application of her remedy small pieces of glass were seen to drop out, at the second, still more, and, at the last, all fell out, and not one was left! This gave the Prince such relief that he opened his eyes and regained consciousness, but did not recognise in the new Hakeem, dressed as a Fakir, his former friend, the Princess. At last he got well, and was able to leave his room, so the Princess went to the Rajah, and begged permission to return to her own country.

"Return to your country when I can give you land and riches and honour here! Why need you do that? Ask me for anything, O wise Hakeem, even for my throne and my kingdom, and you shall have it."

"I desire nothing, O King," returned the poor Hakeem, "but would crave of you a few tokens in remembrance of your son. A handkerchief, his sword, a ring from his finger, and his bow and arrows."

"These gifts are too small a return for all you have done. You shall have them, and much more, if you will."

But the Hakeem refused, and, returning to her home with the tokens she had asked for, once more resumed the dress of a Princess, and, taking out her fan, began to wave it. Immediately the Prince stood in her presence, but she feigned anger with him.

"All these many days I have waved my fan, and you have not come! Why have you come to-day, O Prince?"

Then the Prince told her of all that had happened, of her sisters' cruelty, of his dangerous illness, and of the wonderful Hakeem who had saved his life, and to whom he should ever be grateful. The Princess was glad indeed to hear all this from his own lips, and, bringing out each gift, laid it before his astonished eyes, while she confessed that it was she herself who had tended him in his illness. The Prince was overcome with joy and gratitude, and asked her to become his wife; so they were married amid great feastings and rejoicings, and lived happily ever after. Such is the power of fate.

THE OLD WITCH WHO LIVED IN A FOREST

There was once a Brahmin who had five daughters, and after their mother died, he married another woman who was very unkind to them, and treated them cruelly, and starved them. So stingy was she that, upon one occasion, she took a grain of linseed, divided it into five pieces, and gave a piece to each child.

"Are you satisfied, sister?" they asked one another, and each replied: "I am satisfied," except the youngest, who said: "I am hungry still." Then the eldest, who had still a morsel of the linseed in her mouth, took it and gave it to her little sister.

Soon after their stepmother said to her husband: "These children must be sent away, or else I will go."

He did his best to dissuade her, but she insisted; so, taking the five girls, he went with them to the river, where he suggested they should all cross over to the other side.

"Father, you go first, and we will follow you."

"No, my children, you go first, and I will follow; but, if you should see this umbrella which I carry floating upon the water, you will know that I am drowned and cannot come."

So the children crossed over, and waited for him; but soon, to their grief, they saw the umbrella floating down the stream, and then they knew that their father had been drowned.

After this they wandered about for many days, and passed through many cities. At last they came to a house in the woods, where a woman was sitting. She seemed very pleased to meet them, and invited them indoors; they went in, little knowing that she was a witch, and meant evil. Next day she told them to go and fetch wood, but kept back the eldest to sweep the house, and to keep her company.

In the evening when the other sisters returned, they found their eldest sister was missing; and the witch, who did not wish them to know that she had eaten the child, told them that she had run back to her

THE OLD WITCH WHO LIVED IN A FOREST

"O Tree, shelter me!"

[*To face page 32.*

parents. The next day she did the same thing, and detained the second sister, and so on until only the youngest was left.

At last the old witch told her to stay at home that day to sweep the house, and look after it while she went out. The child swept the room, and then, out of curiosity, opened a box which stood in the corner, and, to her horror, she saw inside it the four heads of her sisters! They were all smiling, and she said: "Why do you smile, O my sisters?"

"Because you will also come here to-day," they replied. The poor child was much alarmed, and asked what she could do to escape.

"Take all the things in this room, and tie them in a bundle, and as you run, throw them on the road. When the old witch comes to look for you, she will see the things, and, while she is picking them up, you will have time to escape." The child quickly did as the heads told her, tied the bundle, and ran away.

There was only a broom left in the room, and when the old witch returned she mounted upon it, and flew through the air in hot pursuit. As she went along she found her things strewn on the road, and began picking them up one after another. This gave the child time to run further and further away, until, at last, she came to a peepul tree, and said: "O tree, shelter me!" and the tree opened, and she was hidden within it, all but her little finger, which remained outside, as the tree closed. This the old witch saw and promptly bit off: while she ate it, she regretted more than once that such a dainty morsel had escaped, but she knew there was no getting out the child; so she went away disappointed.

Now, soon after, a man came to cut down the tree, but the child cried from inside: "Cut above, and cut below, but do not touch the middle, or you will cut me in half."

The voice so amazed the man that he went and told the Rajah about it; and forthwith the Rajah came with all his retinue, and heard the same thing; so they did as the voice advised, and, after carefully opening the tree, found the child, a beautiful young girl, who sat with her hands folded within.

"Girl," said the Rajah, "will you walk

up to anybody here present to whose caste you belong?"

The girl came out and walked up to a Brahmin: this decided the question of her birth, and that she was fitted to become the wife of a Prince. So the Rajah had her taken to his Palace, where they were afterwards married with great pomp, and lived happily ever after.

Note.—It may interest my readers to know that the little native girl standing beside the peepul tree in my sketch is still living. She came to us during one of the great Indian famines, and we almost despaired of her life, for although seven years old at that time, she was a living skeleton, her calf measurement being exactly three-and-a-half inches, or *half of my wrist*! She is now a fine healthy child, and very devoted.—A.E.D.

KULLOO, A FAITHFUL DOG

A CERTAIN Bunniah or merchant married a woman of his own caste, and set out to a distant city. On the way he fell ill with a headache, so she sat by the wayside and pressed his head. While doing so a man passed by, and asked for a little fire to light his *cheelum* for a smoke, but she replied: "I cannot leave my husband, for I am holding his head while he sleeps."

"Put some clothes under his head, and he will sleep," advised the stranger. This she did, but, while giving the fire to the man, he seized her, and, placing her upon his horse, rode away. When the Bunniah awoke, it was to find himself all alone but for his faithful dog Kulloo.

"Master," said Kulloo, "let us become Fakirs, and beg from door to door." So they set out to beg, and one day came to the house of the robber who had stolen the

Bunniah's wife; and she, not recognising her husband or his dog, gave them money and food. But the dog knew her, and that evening he spoke to his master, and asked him if he too had seen his wife. The Bunniah had not; and, guided by Kulloo, he set out to find her.

When they arrived at the robber's house, and made themselves known, the woman was greatly vexed, for the robber was rich, and gave her a very comfortable home; but she pretended to be friendly and invited her husband to dine there that night, telling him that, afterwards, when he had the chance, he could kill the robber.

When the Bunniah had gone, she and the robber arranged a trap for him. It was a hole in the floor, very large and deep, with spikes fixed in the sides of it, so that anybody who fell in might die. Over the hole they set a large brass thalee or plate, so that, while the Bunniah leaned heavily upon it to eat his food, both it and he would fall into the hole.

All happened as they anticipated; and when the poor Bunniah found himself in a deep hole, full of spikes, he thought his last hour had come. But faithful Kulloo came to his rescue, and, taking out the spikes with his teeth, soon set his master free.

The Bunniah then lost no time in seeking the robber, and found him lying fast asleep; so he killed him, and cut off his head, then, taking his wife with him, left the place.

Kulloo followed closely, and licked up each drop of blood which fell from the robber's head, lest it might leave a trace of the deed, and get his master into trouble. He was a wise dog, and knew the woman was wicked, so she hated him, and made up her mind that she would neither eat nor drink until he was dead.

The Bunniah enquired why she would not touch any food, and she told him she would only do so if he killed Kulloo. This the man refused to do; but, after a while, he consented. Poor Kulloo, when he knew his last hour had come, besought his master to bury him carefully, and to see that his head, which the Bunniah meant to cut off, was buried with him, for a time was yet to come when he would again save his master's life.

After Kulloo was dead and buried the wicked woman was happy, and ate and drank as before; but, after a few days, she went and gave notice at the Court that the Bunniah was a cruel robber, who had killed her husband, and stolen her away. The police seized him, and he was taken up for murder; but, just as the Judge was about to pronounce the sentence of death upon him, he remembered faithful Kulloo; and at the same moment the dog appeared!

All were surprised when he stood before the Judge, and asked leave to speak. He then told the whole story of the robber and the wicked woman; and thus, for a second time, saved his master's life, but, having said his say, poor Kulloo disappeared and was never seen again.

THE STORY OF GHOSE

THERE was once a Ranee who had no children, so she made a great pet of a young squirrel, and fed it day after day. One day it entered her head to deceive the Rajah, so she told him that, before the end of the year, an heir would be born in the Palace.

On the appointed day she sent her own nurse (whom she had bribed) to tell the Rajah that the child was born, and was a daughter. The old Brahmin of the Palace hastened to see the young Princess, who was, in reality, no child, but the tame squirrel; so the Ranee persuaded him to go and tell the Rajah that he was now the father of a most lovely daughter: but the stars pointed out that he must not look on her face for twelve years, for, if she looked at him, he would die, and, if he looked at her, she would die. The poor Rajah had no choice but to agree, and thus the Ranee kept up her deception for twelve years, and hid her pet squirrel from everybody.

At last, when the twelve years were over, she said one day to her husband: "Do not look upon your daughter's face till she is married, lest evil come upon her, but go you and make arrangements to marry her to a Prince of good family."

So they sent the old Brahmin to seek for a husband for her; and he went from place to place, until he came to a city where there was a Rajah who had seven sons, all of whom were married but the youngest, whose name was Shahzadah; so the Brahmin chose him, and all was prepared for the marriage.

There was a great feast held, and great rejoicings daily took place in the Palace. When at last the dooly or litter came, for the bride to be carried to her home, the Ranee hid the squirrel inside it, and nobody guessed that there was, in reality, no bride.

On reaching his home the young bridegroom had the dooly placed at the door of his zenana, according to Oriental custom, so that none might see his bride enter; and great indeed was his surprise, when he looked inside, to find nobody there but a squirrel.

For very shame he held his peace, and

told nobody of it, but gave orders in the Palace that he and his wife would live apart by themselves; and she would be in such strict purdah, that even the women of the household would not be allowed to visit her. This gave great offence to everybody; but they put it down to his jealousy, owing to his wife's great beauty, and obeyed.

At last his other brother's wife rebelled, and said: "I refuse to do all the household work; your wife must also take her share in it."

Shahzadah was now very sad, for he felt the time had come for his secret to be discovered, and he would become the laughing-stock of the whole Palace.

The squirrel, who was a great favourite of his, noticed his sadness, and asked him the cause of it. "Why are you sad, O Prince?"

"I am sad because they say you must do some of the household work; and how are you to do it, being only a squirrel?"

"What is it they want me to do?"

"To *leepo* or plaster the floor."

"Well, tell them to do their own portion of the work, and leave me to do mine at my leisure."

This was done, and at night the squirrel went and dipped her tail into the limewash and plaster, and soon had the room better done than the other Ranees.

In the morning all the household were surprised to see the clever way in which Shahzadah's wife had done her work, and they said: "No wonder you hide your wife, when she is so clever."

The next day the task was to grind some corn, and again Shahzadah's heart was heavy, for how could a squirrel turn a heavy stone handmill, and grind corn? But the squirrel said as before: "Tell them to do their work, and to leave mine alone. I will do it when I have finished my bath."

When night came, she went into the room, and with her sharp little teeth, *kutter, kutter, kutter*, soon reduced the corn to powder.

Shahzadah was very pleased with her, and so were they all, and nothing more was said until the next day, when the allotted task was to make a native dish called *goolgoolahs*. This is done by mixing *goor*, or molasses, with flour and water, and frying it in *ghee*, or oil, like fritters.

The poor little squirrel was indeed at her wits' end how to perform the task, for how could so small an animal make so difficult a dish? She tried, and she tried, but failed each time in her attempts, until it was nearly morning.

Just then the God Mahadeo and his wife Parbatti were taking a walk in the dawning light of day. Parbatti saw the poor little squirrel's efforts, and said to Mahadeo: "I will not rest content till you turn that small creature into a human being, so that she can perform her task."

At first Mahadeo refused, but, after a time, he took out a knife, and, making a cut in his finger, took the blood from it, and sprinkled it upon the squirrel, who forthwith turned into a most beautiful Princess.

Just then, as she sat finishing her task, other members of the Royal Family awoke, and came in; they were greatly amazed at her beauty, and led her by the hand to their own apartments.

Meantime, Shahzadah, her husband, was stricken with grief, thinking his poor little squirrel had been burnt to death. He sought her everywhere, and when he could not find her, began to cry: "O my Ghose, my Ghose, where are you?"

The women standing there scolded him for this, and said: "Why do you call your beautiful wife a young squirrel? She is not dead, but has at last been found by us, and is with the other Princesses in the Palace."

But Shahzadah, who knew nothing of what had happened, only wept the more, for he thought they were making fun of him, so he went to his own room, where he flung himself on his couch, and continued to weep. At last he looked up and saw, standing beside him, a beautiful girl, who said: "Do not weep, O Prince, for I am your squirrel." Then she told him all that had happened.

This was indeed good news, and it was not long before the grateful Princess wrote to her foster-mother, who had been so good and kind to her when she was only a helpless little creature, and invited her and her father the Rajah to come on a visit. This was the first time the Rajah had seen or kissed his daughter, and he was indeed pleased to find she was so beautiful. So there were great rejoicings in the Palace, and they all lived happily ever after.

THE VIZIER'S SON AND THE RAJAH'S SON

The Vizier's and the Rajah's son were great friends, and always together. This made the Rajah very jealous, and he called an old woman whom he knew, and asked her to separate the two.

This was a difficult task, as they were such fast friends, but the old woman was anxious to gain a reward, and said she would do it; so she called the Vizier's son, and when he asked her what she required, remained silent. Then she called the Rajah's son, and did the same.

After she had gone, the two questioned each other as to what she had said, and neither would believe the other when he declared she had said nothing at all; so they began to suspect one another of deceit, and quarrelled.

Thus the old woman sowed dissension in their hearts, and after a time, instead of being friends, they became bitter enemies. The

Rajah's son said he insisted on knowing what the old woman had said to the Vizier's son, and if he would not tell it, he must be put to death at the hands of a sweeper, or, in India, low-caste man.

The sweeper was just about to do this cruel deed, when the Goddess Parbatti saw him, and implored of Mahadeo, her husband, to intercede; so he sent a large stag to the jungle, and it stood near at hand.

When the sweeper saw it, he killed it instead with the bow and arrows, and, taking out its eyes, carried them to the Rajah, and said they were the eyes of the Vizier's son.

Thus the Prince was appeased, and again ate, drank, and was merry, until one day, walking in the garden, he saw an earthen vessel, and in it a lock of hair and a small lamp. This, he felt sure, had some significance, so he longed to ask the Vizier's son, who was clever, and would have told him all about it; but he remembered that the Vizier's son was taken away and killed, and he himself had seen his eyes brought back in proof of the deed.

Nevertheless he wept day and night, and would not be comforted, so the Rajah, his father, in great distress, sent for the sweeper who had been told to kill the Vizier's son, and implored him to declare the truth concerning his end. Then the man confessed everything, and went and searched for the lad, and brought him back. The two boys became fast friends as before, and the Rajah's son enquired the meaning of the lock of woman's hair and lamp.

"It means," said the Vizier's son, "the name of a beautiful Princess called 'Princess of the Lamp,' and she lives in a distant country."

So they set out to seek her, and soon found the Palace in which she lived, and outside a girl making a wreath of flowers for the Princess. The Rajah's son begged the girl to let *him* make the *hal* or wreath, and, in making it, he placed a letter inside.

The Princess was very angry when she found the letter, and made the girl tell her the truth; but she would not receive the Prince after what he had done, so he had to return to his own country: thus was he punished for his cruelty to the Vizier's son.

THE RAJAH'S SON AND THE VIZIER'S SON

For a second time the friendship of the Rajah's son and the Vizier's son caused great jealousy, so a mischief-maker was called, and he promised he would do all in his power to part them. Then he ordered a dooly and followed them into the forest. At the first opportunity he called to the eldest, who was the Vizier's son, and pretended to whisper in his ear.

The Rajah's son at once enquired what the man had said, and would not believe that it was nothing at all, so once again in great anger he ordered his friend to be killed.

But the Vizier's son was very clever, and soon persuaded the executioner to spare his life, for he told him the Rajah's son would very soon weary of being alone, and would ask for him back; and if the executioner could not bring him, he would most probably suffer death himself; thus he escaped, and went and hid himself.

In the meantime the Rajah's son chanced to walk by the riverside, where he saw a very beautiful woman sitting beside her husband. He admired the woman very much, and communicated his feelings in looks, though he dared not do so in words.

The woman replied by first spreading a little green plaster on the ground, on which she placed a brass vessel, or *lota*, and over that another or smaller lota, on the top of which was a looking-glass, with ashes spread upon it.

The Rajah's son looked carefully at what she had done, but could not interpret its meaning, so he bitterly regretted the death of his friend, who was noted for his cleverness, and went at once to the executioner to enquire about him.

The executioner owned that he had not killed the boy, and went and called him. Then the friends went together to discover what the woman meant, nor was the Vizier's son long in finding the meaning.

The green plaster meant, "In a green spot lives Lota (the name of her husband), and Gudba (or smaller vessel) is the name of the city where we live; the looking-glass means in a house which has many glasses in it; and the ashes mean, 'May these ashes be on your head if you fail to discover my meaning.'"

After this clue, it did not take the Vizier's son long to find out where the woman lived, and he put pegs into the wall, one above the other, for his friend to climb up to her window.

But before the Rajah's son could reach the top, a Kotwal, or policeman, saw him, and took him away to the lock-up. This was an unexpected turn of affairs, so the Vizier's son quickly dressed himself as a beautiful woman, and asked to see his friend in the prison. He bribed the jailer to let him in, and, once there, made his friend put on his clothes and escape, while he remained prisoner in his stead.

Next day the news went abroad that the Kotwal had locked up both the Rajah's son and the Vizier's son in the prison, and the Rajah was very angry about it, and sent at once to find out the reason.

They determined to put the matter as to who was innocent and who was guilty to a test; so the Kotwal had a pan of boiling oil prepared, and said who ever plunged his hand into it, who was innocent of crime, would not be burnt.

Each dipped his hand in turn, the Rajah's son, the Vizier's son, the woman, and the Kotwal himself, but only the Kotwal had his hand badly burnt, so this ended the whole affair. The Rajah's son meantime had dressed himself as a woman, and taken service in the house of the beautiful woman who was the wife of a Sowcar.

Nobody guessed who he was, until one day the Sowcar himself admired him, and tried to be friends with him, thinking he was only a pretty servant-girl; then the Sowcar's wife gave her pretended servant-girl a razor, and said to keep it carefully till the next time the Sowcar came to see her, and then to cut off his nose.

The Rajah's son, who was tired of acting the part of a servant-girl, was only too glad to do this; and the Sowcar, rather than let anybody know of his disgrace in having lost his nose, left the country, and thus his wife gained her ends.

BEY HUSLO

Bey Huslo was a very extravagant woman, who was always being found fault with by her husband, who held up as her examples other women who were thrifty in their habits, and who saved money, and helped to make and build up their husbands' homes.

On hearing this Bey Huslo took a pick-axe, and began digging here and there like a mason. Her husband asked what she was doing, and she replied: "Trying to build you a house."

He tried to explain that that was not literally meant, and explained again the duties of a wife. "When a good wife falls short of supplies, she borrows two *cuttorah's* full (or small earthen vessels full) of flour from her neighbour, and thus saves herself the expense of buying any large quantity."

That night Bey Huslo, who had taken this saying literally, borrowed two small earthen vessels, and, breaking them into small pieces, put them on the fire to cook!

Her husband heard the sound as they grated against the cooking-pot, and asked what she was cooking that made such a noise; but he was very angry indeed when she told him, and scolded her roundly.

He told her she was perfectly useless, and that, while he had to go about without clothes, other women were able to spin and weave. She replied that if he would only give her some wool, she could do the same.

The man was delighted, and gave her some wool; so she took it to the pond, and told the frogs and toads to weave it into cloth for her.

After some days her husband asked her if the cloth was ready, and she said: "I gave it to the frogs and toads to weave for me, and find they have not done so."

Then her husband was very angry indeed, and said: "Senseless one, have you ever heard of frogs and toads spinning cloth? Go out of my house this moment!" And, with that, he turned her out, and she went and climbed up into a peepul tree.

Soon after some camels came that way,

and, as they stretched out their necks and ate the branches, Bey Huslo called out: "Go away, I will not go with you; I will only go when my husband comes to fetch me."

But as the camels had only come to eat, and not to fetch her, they made no reply, and went away.

After this a dog began to bark at her, but she said again: "Go away, I will not go with you; I will only go with my husband."

When night fell some thieves sat sharing their spoils under the tree, and Bey Huslo felt so frightened that she fell off, and dropped in their midst.

The thieves did not know what to make of it, and ran away, leaving their stolen property behind. Bey Huslo soon gathered it up and returned to her husband. "Here," she said, "is more than enough for you and for me. We will now live at our ease, and I will have no housekeeping to do, so that you can no longer call me a worthless wife."

THE STORY OF PANCH MAR KHAN

THERE was once a weaver who had the habit of slapping his face to kill any flies that settled upon it; and it was rumoured that he killed five at every blow, so he got the name of Panch Mar Khan, which means "a killer of five."

People did not know that this name applied to flies, but thought the weaver a brave, strong man, able to kill five of his enemies at a blow, so that he gained a reputation for bravery.

One day the Rajah of that place heard some enemies were coming in force to attack his capital. All the fighting men were required to go out and meet them on the morrow; so Panch Mar Khan received notice to be in readiness also.

Now he had never touched a weapon in his life, and was horribly frightened at the very idea, so he made up his mind to run away during the night.

He saddled his donkey, and, taking two large millstones, set out on his journey; but, as he was passing the enemy's camp, and arrived at a hill just a little above it, the donkey began to kick and to bray, and the two stones rolled down the hill into the enemy's camp with a great noise.

They thought an army was after them, and became terror-stricken, so that in the darkness and panic which ensued, many of them were killed.

Panch Mar Khan was greatly delighted at his good luck, and, instead of running away, returned to his own home.

Next morning, when the soldiers came to call him out to fight the enemy, he very proudly asked: "What enemy? Did I not go out at night, and kill hundreds of our enemies and drive the rest away?"

True enough, there was now no camp to be seen, and several dead men were found on the spot; so Panch Mar Khan's reputation as a brave man spread far and wide, and he was handsomely rewarded by the Rajah.

Some days after news came that a tiger was prowling about; and a brave man was required to go out that night and kill it.

Who was so brave as Panch Mar Khan! So he was deputed to go, but when he heard this he nearly died of fright, and made up his mind that he would run away.

So when darkness fell he crept out and caught his donkey by the ear, and led it to its stable, and there tied it to a post, to wait till he was ready to get on its back; but when he returned with a light, what was his surprise to find it was not his donkey, but the tiger that he had led by the ear and tied to a post.

Such brave conduct from a mortal to a wild beast had so amazed the tiger, that it was too frightened to resist, so there it remained till morning, and Panch Mar Khan was thought to be the bravest man alive!

Next morning he got up early, and went out into the field near his house, and there he suddenly came face to face with the fierce eyes and grinning teeth of a jackal. His other bravery was by mistake, but this was a reality, and so frightened was he, that he fell down and died on the spot.

THE RABBIT AND THE BARBER

There was a rabbit who asked a barber to shave him; in doing so the barber cut off his ear. "Take my ear," said the rabbit, "and I will take your razors."

A little further on he saw an old woman pulling grass with her hands. "Take this," he said, giving her the razor, "and cut grass with it, and I will take your cloth."

When she asked him why, he replied: "You have my razor and I have your chudder."

Then he went a little further and saw a ghee seller. "Take my chudder and give me your ghee," said the rabbit. So saying, he left the chudder and walked off with the ghee.

Not long after he met a woman, and told her to make him some *goolgoolahs*, or sweets, with the ghee. As soon as they were ready he picked them up and ran away.

A little further on was a man with a plough, a horse, and a bullock. "Take these sweets," said the rabbit, "and I will yoke your plough for you."

But, instead of doing this, he ran away with the horse, and soon after met a marriage procession, in which the bridegroom was walking beside the bride's litter or dooly. "Get on my horse: why do you walk?" said the rabbit gaily.

So the man got on, and the rabbit ran off with the bride; but her husband ran after, and advised his wife to kill the rabbit.

When they got to a quiet place, and rested under a tree, she asked the rabbit to let her comb his hair; but as soon as he put his head down, she gave him a severe knock on it, which stunned him, and then ran back to her husband. Thus ended the adventures of the rabbit.

RUPA AND BISUNTHA

There was once a woman who had no little children of her own; every day she used to watch the sparrows building their nests, and bringing up their young, and it so happened that one day a mother bird died, leaving several young ones. After a time a new mother bird was brought, and she was not at all good to the young fledglings.

The woman felt hurt for them, and said to her husband: "If I had children of my own, and after a time I died, would you do as the birds have done, and let my children be unkindly treated?"

But the man replied: "These are birds, and I am a man."

After some years the woman had two sons, and when they had grown to be big boys, she died. Her husband had forgotten her conversation about the birds, and he married another wife.

One day the eldest boy was playing with a ball, when it fell into his stepmother's room. He asked if he might fetch it; but when he went inside, she made it an occasion for all sorts of complaints against him to his father, so his father turned him out of the house, and he went away with his little brother.

As they rested that night in the forest, the younger brother lay awake and overheard a conversation between two Night Jars. They talked on many subjects. At length one of the birds remarked: "How little do people guess that he who eats me will become a Rajah, and he who eats you will become a Prime Minister."

On hearing this the youngest brother crept out of bed, and taking his gun, shot both birds and cooked them. He ate the female himself, and kept the male for his brother. But while he slept, a venomous snake, which lived in the tree, came down and bit him, so that he died as he slept.

In the morning his elder brother awoke, and found a meal prepared for him, so he ate the bird, and then tried to wake his companion, but soon discovered that the boy was dead. This grieved him very much, and he wept bitterly, and determined to wait till he could return and burn his brother in a way befitting to a good caste Hindu, so he placed him in the branches of the tree and went his way.

The same day Mahadeo and Parbatti were passing that way, and Parbatti, who is ever described as a wilful Goddess, always wanting her own way, asked Mahadeo to see what was in the tree. They soon found the dead boy; and Parbatti insisted that he should be made alive again, so Mahadeo sprinkled a few drops of blood upon him, and he sat up alive and well.

Close to this place a Rajah had just died, and his people placed his crown in the trunk of an elephant, leaving it to him to place it upon the head of any man there; and that man would be their future King. The elephant looked upon them all, and then, walking up to Rupa, placed the crown upon his head.

At first the people objected, because he was a stranger, and did not belong to their town, but after a while they accepted him as their King, and thus the words of the bird were fulfilled.

In the meantime, Bisuntha came to the same city, and begged a night's shelter. The people were fully aware that night after night a fierce man-eating tiger came to that town, and demanded a man to eat. They did not wish to give one of the men belonging to the town, so Bisuntha, being a stranger, was selected for the tiger, and told to go and sleep in the place where it was likely to come.

At night he lay awake thinking, and the tiger came; but Bisuntha had his sword beside him, so he promptly killed the tiger, and placed its ears and whiskers in his pocket.

In the morning a sweeper came, thinking to find the stranger dead and his bones scattered about, but, instead, he found the tiger dead, and the stranger lying fast asleep; so he resolved to take all the honour of killing the tiger to himself, and went back to the city with the news that he had killed the tiger single-handed, and saved the man. This story was believed, and the sweeper richly rewarded, but Bisuntha heard nothing.

Now there lived in that city a merchant who owned a ship and went to distant cities to trade, but sometimes the ship stuck in the sandbanks, and could not be moved. At such times it was necessary to kill a man, and then the sand was pleased at the sacrifice and let the ship go. It was always difficult to find a man for the purpose, and the Rajah was often asked to select one.

Bisuntha, at this time, had taken up service in the house of an oil merchant, and being a stranger, he was selected for a second time, and sent by the Rajah to accompany the merchant, at the risk of his life.

At the first sandbank, when the ship was in difficulties and could not be moved, the merchant told Bisuntha he must prepare to die; but Bisuntha said: "You desire your ship to move, whether I die or whether I do not. If I can make it move on for you, will you spare my life?"

To this the merchant agreed; and Bisuntha cut his finger, and dropped a few drops of blood into the sea. As soon as he did this the ship moved on, and so the merchant would not part with him, or kill him, but kept him during the whole voyage, and brought him back to the town.

Rupa had half forgotten his brother all this while, but one day he was stricken with remorse, and determined to find out what had happened after he had left the forest, with the intention of burning the remains of Bisuntha.

In order to get news of him, he sent out a notice that he would pay any one who would come daily and talk with him, for he hoped in the course of conversation that some one would mention the circumstance of the boy who was found dead in a tree in the forest.

At length Bisuntha himself came to hear what the Rajah his brother was doing, so he disguised himself as a girl, and went to the Palace.

When the Rajah saw him he said: "What have you to say, O my daughter?" and Bisuntha said: "Do you wish me to talk on general subjects or only of myself?"

"Of yourself," said Rupa.

So the lad began. "There were once two brothers, whose names were Rupa and Bisuntha, and they had a stepmother."

Rupa's interest was now breathless, but after telling a small part of the story Bisuntha said he was tired, and would tell the rest next day.

The next day he continued, and told how a snake had bitten Bisuntha, and how he had died in the forest, and had been raised to life by Mahadco and Parbatti. Rupa was now full of anxiety to know the rest, but Bisuntha said he had forgotten it, so nothing could be done.

When he came again, he said he remembered that Bisuntha came to a certain town, where the Rajah ordered him to be given to a tiger; how he had escaped the tiger and all other dangers, and had in his pocket the proof. Thus saying he took out the tiger's ears and whiskers, and, as his eyes met his brother's, they recognised each other, and fell upon each other's necks.

SHEIK CHILLI

THE hero of this story was one day walking along with a vessel of oil upon his head. As he walked he kept thinking of the future.

"I will sell the oil, and with the money I shall buy a goat, and then I shall sell the kids, and then I shall buy a cow, and sell the milk, till I get a large sum of money; then I shall buy a pair of buffaloes, and a field, and plough the field, and gain more money, and build myself a house, and marry a wife, and have many sons and daughters. And when my wife comes to call me to dinner, I'll say: 'Dhur, away! I'll come when I think fit!'" and with that he held up his head suddenly, and away fell the *chattie* with the oil, and it was all spilt.

This upset Sheik Chilli so much that he began to yell: "I have lost my goats, I have lost my cows, I have lost my buffaloes, and my house, and my wife and children."

That such dire calamity should befall a

Sheik Chilli
"I've lost my goats, I've lost my cows!"

[To face page 68.

man caused great pity, so the bystanders took Sheik Chilli to the Rajah, who asked him how it had all happened.

When he heard the story he laughed, and said: "This boy has a good heart, let him be given a reward to compensate him for the loss of his oil."

SHEIK CHILLI

SHEIK CHILLI was going to be married, so his mother said: "My son, whatever your wife gives you to eat be content with your *nemak panee* (literally salt and water, but a native always speaks of his food as his "nemak panee"), and do not grumble, but eat uncomplaining."

So when he was married, and his wife placed his food before him, he remembered his mother's warning, and kept repeating, "Nemak panee, nemak panee," till his wife was disgusted, and taking him at his word gave him salt and water to drink.

During the night he felt very hungry, and asked her to give him some food, but she said: "I am not going to get up and cook food for you at this hour of the night, but if you will go into a certain room, you will find some honey in a jar on the shelf, eat a little of that."

Sheik Chilli, in trying to reach the jar of

honey, upset it, and it came pouring down upon him, while he kept calling out, "Stop, stop, I've had enough," till at last, surfcited with honey and smeared with it from head to foot, he returned to his wife, and told her what had happened. She advised him to go into the next room, where he would find some wool, and clean himself with it.

He tried to do this, but the wool stuck fast to the honey, and covered his body and his hands, so that he looked more like a sheep than a man, and his wife told him that he had better go and sleep with the sheep until morning, when she would prepare some warm water for him to have a wash.

That night some thieves came to steal the sheep, and in the darkness they felt each one to see which was fattest. Sheik Chilli was fast asleep, and they thought he was a very fine sheep; so they put him into a bag and ran away, taking him with them. When he awoke he kept calling out: "Let me go, let me go." This frightened the robbers, who had never heard a sheep call out before, and so they put down the bag and out dropped Sheik Chilli.

The robbers asked him who he was, and

said: "You must come with us now, for we are just going to rob the house of a very rich Bunniah; while we gather the spoils, you keep watch that he does not wake."

Sheik Chilli waited patiently till he thought the robbers were ready to run away; and then he dropped some hot rice, that was in the cooking pot on the fire, upon the hand of the Bunniah's wife. She awoke with a scream, and the robbers ran away. Then Sheik Chilli explained how he had saved the Bunniah from great loss, and was allowed to go free without any more questions being asked.

When he got outside he saw a camel laden with all sorts of treasure. The camel-driver had turned aside for a minute or so, and Sheik Chilli could not see him, so he lead off the camel, made over its pack to his mother, and let it walk away empty.

Next day there was a great fuss made, and the town-crier went round to say that a camel had strayed, and certain valuable goods were lost.

Sheik Chilli's mother heard this, and knowing how simple her son was, she feared he would tell every one where the things were, so she resolved to divert his mind, and that night cooked some *goolgoolahs*, a very favourite native dish, like fritters, and flung them into the garden; then she woke her son and told him it was "raining goolgoolahs from the sky!"

The foolish fellow ran out and called to everybody: "It is raining goolgoolahs! it is raining goolgoolahs!" Everybody thought him a fool, and said: "It is that mad Sheik Chilli; who is going to listen to him?"

Next day Sheik Chilli heard the town-crier calling out about the camel, so he promptly said: "My mother has the things; I myself brought the camel to her."

Then they all crowded to his mother's door, and she asked: "On what day did you bring the camel, my son?"

"The day it rained goolgoolahs, mother."

So the people walked away disgusted, and said: "What fool's talk is this? Who ever heard of its raining goolgoolahs? The one statement is as false as the other."

After this his mother advised him to return to his wife, who must wonder what had become of him. "And mind," she said, "whatever your wife may say, you must agree, and say 'Acchābat'"—or "Quite right," as we English would say "Good!" or "Very good news!"

So he returned to his wife, and the first piece of news she gave him was that her mother had been put into prison, to which he replied, "Acchābat," or "Very good." On this his wife was exceedingly vexed, and turned him out of the house.

He returned to his mother, who asked him what had happened. She said: "You are indeed a foolish boy, you should have said, 'Ah ha! Ah ha! this is indeed sad news.' I hope you will remember next time what I have told you."

So Sheik Chilli went back to his wife, who greeted him with the news that his mother-in-law had been released.

"Ah ha!" said Sheik Chilli, "this is indeed sad news."

The mother-in-law, who overheard him, said: "I have had enough of you: take your wife, and go and live in your own mother's house." So she turned him out.

THE MONKEY, THE TIGER, AND THE PRINCESS

Once upon a time there was a King who had seven sons, and he made up his mind that he would not let them marry unless they married seven sisters, so he sent his Brahmin to seek a Rajah who had seven daughters, and to bring him word. After a time the Brahmin succeeded, and found a Rajah who had seven daughters; so arrangements were speedily made for their marriage.

When the time came for the seven Princes to go and fetch their brides, the youngest said to his father: "If we all go, who is to look after the house, and all your property? Let me remain behind, and when my brothers return with their wives, they can bring my bride also."

His father thought this a very wise suggestion, so they set out, leaving the youngest brother at home.

After the wedding festivities were over,

the seven brides were carried along in doolies, with the six Princes for an escort, and they halted for the night near a tank or pond in the forest, but did not know that the place was full of tigers. At night the tigers formed a ring round the camp, and said they would eat every one in it unless one of the Princesses was given up to them.

None of the six Princes would give up his wife. At last they decided to leave the seventh Princess to the tigers.

When the procession arrived at the Rajah's Palace, the youngest Prince wondered why only six doolies had come, and asked what had become of his bride; but nobody would give him an answer.

At last an old man told him what had happened, and the young Prince, who was very angry and disappointed with his brothers, at once set out to seek his bride.

On the way he met a rat and a jackal, and they said: "May we go with you?" The Prince consented, and the three set out together, and walked or rode till evening, when they were overcome with fatigue and sat down to rest.

The Prince fell asleep, but the jackal said

to the rat: "I am very hungry, what shall we do for food? Do you eat the Prince's clothes, and I will eat his horse."

No sooner did they agree than they carried out their plan. The rat ate all the clothes worn by the Prince, and the jackal ate his horse, so that when he awoke it was to find himself alone in the forest, without either horse or clothes.

Just then a monkey came down from the tree, and asked him what was the matter.

"I have told my troubles to two animals before, and do not wish to be betrayed by a third," said the Prince; to which the monkey replied: "A rat is a rat, and a jackal is a jackal, but I am a monkey; come with me and I will help you out of your troubles."

Then they went to the Bazaar, where the monkey gave his friend the Prince some money, and told him to buy himself clothes. When he had bought the clothes, he gave him some more money and said to buy himself a sword and ornaments, and lastly to buy himself a horse, and the monkey advised that it should be a thin horse, fleet of limb.

Then the two mounted the horse and rode into the forest, where they soon found the

Princess sitting tied up in a den, with an old blind tiger in charge of her. The blind tiger held two strings; one was attached to the girl, and the other to a large tiger who had gone out with the rest of the tigers, but who, at the slightest pull of the string, was ready to return to give any assistance required of him.

The monkey whispered to the girl to try and free herself, and meantime, he began to sweep the room, and busy himself, so that the old blind tiger might think the girl was busy at her household work.

After a time the girl managed to get away, and she fled with the Prince, until the monkey thought they were at a safe distance; then he turned round and dealt several blows to the old blind tiger, who, in her turn, pulled the string. A great big tiger at once came to her assistance, and asked what had happened, but he was enraged to find that the girl had gone, and beat the old tiger soundly, before setting off in hot pursuit.

On the way he saw a man, who was in reality the monkey in disguise, sitting beside a funeral pyre.

"What is this for?" asked the tiger.

"A certain tiger," said the monkey, "has killed his mother to-day, and this is to burn her upon."

The tiger felt remorse, for he had not meant to kill the old tiger, so he rushed back to the den, and this gave the fugitives time to escape yet further; but when the tiger found his mother alive and well, he was so angry that he dragged her out of the den by her feet and threw her on the ground.

Then he ran back to where the monkey was sitting and found him still busy with the funeral pyre, for he said that an old woman had been dragged out by her feet that day, and she was even now being carried to be burnt.

The tiger was filled with remorse at what he had done, and for a second time ran back to the den. By this time both the Prince and the Princess had escaped in safety, and the monkey joined them.

They were always good to him, but he pined for the woods and the forests; yet, whenever he asked to be allowed to return, they would not allow it. So one day he determined to make the Princess so angry that she would herself turn him out. He awaited his opportunity, and broke all the thread as she was spinning. The Princess threw something heavy at his head, and he feigned to fall down dead.

Great were the lamentations over the faithful monkey, and he was carried in solemn ceremony to be burnt, just as though he were a Rajah's son; but the moment they laid him upon the fire, up he jumped, and ran off.

The Princess scolded him for causing her such sorrow, but he explained that since there was no other way of getting back into the forest and regaining his liberty, he had thought this the best way. Then they all came home, and let the monkey sport in the forest as before.

THE JACKAL AND THE GUANA

A JACKAL once made itself a throne of bones near the river-side, and levied toll on all the animals that came there to drink water, making each say in turn these words:

> "Golden is your throne,
> Silver is its plaster,
> In your ears are golden earrings,
> And you sit like a Rajah."

This praise pleased the jackal, and he was puffed up with his own importance.

One day a guana, or iguana, a very large lizard, called by the natives "Go," came to the river, but when the jackal asked it to repeat the words, it said: "Let me drink first, for I am dying of thirst;" so he let it drink, and when it had finished, it said:

> "Bones are your throne,
> With cow dung are they plastered,
> In your ears are shoes,
> And you sit like a jackal."

This made the jackal wild with anger, so he ran after the Go to kill it, and caught its tail in his teeth, just as the Go was getting into a hole. "Hoo hoo," said the jackal.

"Don't say Hoo, say Ha," called the Go; so the jackal said "Ha!" and in order to say it, had to open his mouth, so the Go escaped!

THE STORY OF THE BLACK COW

There was a certain Brahmin whose wife died leaving him one little son. For some time the two lived happily together, but at last the Brahmin married for a second time, and the woman, who had a daughter of her own, was very unkind to her little stepson.

Each day the two children went out together to attend to the cattle, and at night they returned home to eat their food. But the cakes made by the Brahmin's wife for her stepson were of ashes, with just a little flour mixed in to give them the appearance of food, that the Brahmin might not notice; and the child ate in silence, for he was afraid to complain, yet, when he was alone in the forest he wept from hunger, and a black cow, one of the herd, saw this, and asked him what was the matter.

The boy told her everything, and presently she beat her hoofs upon the ground. As she did so, sweets of all kinds appeared, which the child ate greedily, and shared with his little sister, warning her the while not to mention at home what the black cow had done, lest the stepmother should be angry.

The stepmother meanwhile wondered to see how well the boy looked, and she resolved to keep watch, for she suspected that he drank the milk while tending her cows; so she told her little daughter to keep a good look-out on all his doings, and to let her know. At last the girl confessed that they ate sweets every day, and the black cow provided the feast.

That day when the Brahmin came home his wife begged him to sell the black cow, and said she would neither sleep nor eat until this was done.

The poor boy was sad indeed when he heard this, and went at once to his favourite, where, throwing himself on the black cow's neck, he wept bitterly.

"Do not weep, my child, but get up on my back, and I will carry you to a place of safety where we can still be together."

So they escaped to a forest, and there lived in peace and security for many days.

Now, in the forest was a hole, which led to the home of the Great Snake, which, together with a bull, holds up the universe. Into this hole the black cow poured five seers of milk daily to feed the snake. This pleased the snake so much that he said one day: "I must go up into the world and see for myself the creature who is so good to me and who sends me such good milk to drink."

When he came he saw the black cow grazing with the boy beside her.

The cow asked no favours for herself, but when the snake asked what she would like, she said she would like her son, as she called the Brahmin's son, to be clothed in gold from head to foot, and that all his body might shine as gold.

This wish the snake readily granted, but both cow and boy afterwards regretted their request, for they feared robbers.

One day as the boy had his bath by the river, and combed his long locks of pure gold, some of his golden hair fell into the water, and was swallowed by a fish. This fish was caught by a fisherman, and taken for sale to the King's Palace. When they cut it open all present admired the lovely golden hair, and when the Princess saw it, she said she would never be happy again until she met the owner. The fisherman was asked where he caught the fish, and people were despatched in all directions in boats to search both far and wide.

At last a man in one of the boats espied in the distance a beautiful shining object taking a bath by the river-side. Little by little the boat came closer and closer, until it was alongside; then the man called out and asked the bather to come a little nearer. At first the Brahmin's son would not listen, but after a time he came up to the boat, when, to his surprise, he was at once seized, tied up, and carried away.

Arrived at the King's Palace he met the Princess, who was very beautiful; and when he saw her he forgot everything else, and thought only of her.

After a short time they were married, and spent many happy days together; but some one chanced to offer them a sweet-meat made of curds, such as the black cow often gave her boy, and in a frenzy of remorse, the Brahmin's son remembered his faithful friend and hastened to the place in the distant forest where he had last seen her. Arrived there he found only a few bones of dead cattle strewn about.

He was heart-broken at the sight, and gathered all the bones together into a funeral pyre, upon which he declared he would lay down his own life; but just as he was about to do this who should appear but his old friend, the black cow.

They were overjoyed to see each other, and she told him she had only kept the bones there to test his affection; but now that she was satisfied that he had not forgotten her, the meeting was full of happiness and joy, so they held a great feast for many days and then went their separate ways as before.

THE BRAHMIN AND THE WILD GEESE

THERE was once a Brahmin who had a large family, and was very poor. Every day he went out into the Bazaar to beg, but whether he begged for only an hour, or for the whole day, he seldom succeeded in getting a seer of *atta* (two pounds of flour).

Now this made his wife very angry, for she thought that the longer he begged, the more he should gain. She suspected that he sold what he was given, instead of bringing it home for his family, so she accused him and beat him soundly.

The Brahmin was deeply vexed at her treatment, and determined to go to the river and there drown himself; yet when he tried to do so, his courage failed, so he alternately threw himself into the water and then changed his mind and came out again.

His conduct attracted the attention of a couple of wild geese, who had their nest near by.

"I wonder what that man is doing; I think I will go and see," said the gander; but his wife advised him not, "for who knows the ways of human beings."

Yet he would not listen, and going up to the Brahmin, asked him the reason of his strange conduct.

The Brahmin told him everything, and when he had done the goose said: "Shut your eyes till I tell you to open them."

The Brahmin did as he was told, and on opening his eyes, the goose held out to him in its beak, a most valuable and beautiful ruby.

"Take this, my friend, and sell it to a Rajah, and then your troubles will be all over."

The Brahmin thanked him warmly, and went off with his treasure to the nearest State; there the Rajah looked at the ruby, but said he could not afford to buy so valuable a gem unless the Brahmin would accept for it seven mule loads of money. This the Brahmin gladly consented to do, and returned to his home a rich man.

Some time after this, the poor Rajah who had bought the ruby got leprosy, and called all the physicians he could find to cure him. One of these said he would be cured if he ate the flesh of a wild goose, and applied its fat to his hands.

That very day the Rajah sent for the Brahmin, and told him to go without delay and fetch him a wild goose, when he would reward him greatly. Now, the Brahmin loved money, and for his greed of gold, forgot all the kindness of the wild goose, and made up his mind to secure it; so he went to the river as before, and began to try and drown himself.

The geese watched him with much concern, for they wondered what had caused this fresh trouble, after all that had been done for him. Perhaps a thief had stolen the ruby. The old gander ran to enquire, but his wife warned him not to go.

"What is the matter, O Brahmin?"

"Nothing, my friend, except that I wish to behold your face again."

"Well, here I am."

"Ah, not so far, my friend; come nearer that I may caress you," cried the Brahmin.

So the foolish bird came nearer, and no sooner had he done so, than the Brahmin seized him and put him in a bag, with only his head out.

As they went along, the poor goose shed bitter tears of reproach, and each tear became a beautiful pearl. The Rajah's son chanced to come that way, saw the pearls, and followed in their track, until he came to the spot where the Brahmin sat.

"What is in your bag?" he asked; "and why do pearls fall from it as you walk along?"

The Brahmin denied that he had anything in his bag, but the Prince would not listen, and accused him of theft; so at length he opened it, and displayed the wild goose. The poor bird told the Prince of all he had done for the Brahmin, and of the poor return and ingratitude he was having now. This made the Prince very angry, and he at once released the goose, who gladly flew away.

The Brahmin then went to the Rajah, and told him what his son had done, and orders were at once given to banish the Prince from the kingdom.

Then the Prince went to the river and told the wild goose of his banishment, and, out of gratitude, the goose and his wife brought food and fruit daily, and placed it before him. This went on for some time, and then the geese decided to find a wife for their visitor.

Now a lovely Princess lived in a Palace close to that place; and one night, while she slept, the two geese joined wings under her bed, and carried her to the river. In the morning when she awoke she was surprised to find herself in this lonely place.

But the Prince met her and told her that he too was banished; and they became great friends and soon afterwards were married. The wild geese gave them many beautiful and valuable gifts, and they went to live in the former home of the Princess.

THE FOUR-GIFTED PRINCESS

THERE was once a King, who was sitting with his wife before the fire when they heard a partridge call. The King said: "That sound comes from the left," and his wife said it came from the right, so they had a bet about it, and the Rajah said: "If you are right you may have my kingdom, and I will cease to reign any longer;" so he went out, and found that his wife was right.

This being the case, he began to make preparations to leave, and to make over his kingdom to her; but, as he was about to do this, his servants, who knew of the bet, advised him not to be so foolish, but to take another wife, and to do away with this one, rather than part with the kingdom. At first the King would not listen, but after a time he agreed to leave the matter in their hands.

That night they waited till the poor Ranee lay asleep, and took her as she slept, placed her in a box, locked it up, and threw it into a river.

An old Fakir was in the habit of bathing in the river very early in the morning, and when he came he found the box and opened it. The Ranee was unconscious, but not dead; so he carried her to his own home, and there looked after her until she recovered.

Now the Ranee was about to present the kingdom with an heir, and was very miserable to find herself deserted and in a strange home at such a time, so she cried bitterly, and three fairies were sent to her assistance.

Soon after this a little daughter was born to her, and when the child was a month old, the three fairies took their leave, but, before going, each determined to leave a parting gift for the little Princess.

The first said that whenever she placed her foot on a stone it would turn to either silver or gold. The second said that whenever she laughed sweet scented flowers would fall from her lips. The third said that whenever she cried pearls would fall from her eyes.

All these things came to pass, so in time they built a beautiful Palace.

One day the Rajah passed that way, and asked the Brahmin how he had built such a lovely Palace in the place of his old mud-hut.

The old man told him how he had found the box, and all about the Queen, his wife, whom he thought was dead.

The Rajah owned his sin, and implored forgiveness of his wife. At first she refused to forgive him, but after a time she listened, and the Rajah said that, if ever again he did anything to vex or hurt her, the old Fakir might punish him as he thought best.

Now the Indian people dread the punishment of a holy Fakir; so the Queen returned to her former Palace, and lived happily ever after.

THE MAN WHO WENT TO SEEK HIS FORTUNE

There was once a Zemindar or Jhut who was very poor, and he had a brother who was very rich, but the rich brother never helped him at all and often reproached him for his poverty.

One day the poor Zemindar determined to go out into the wide world to seek his fortune, and not to return until he had found it.

Having thus made up his mind he set out on his journey, and the first thing he came across was a King's Palace, which was in the hands of carpenters and masons; but no sooner had they built it up on one side, than the other side fell down, so that the place was at all times under repairs, and caused its owner much expense and anxiety.

As the Zemindar stood watching the place, the King came out, and asked him who he

THE MAN WHO WENT TO SEEK HIS FORTUNE

While he stood there the old Fakir opened his eyes and saw him.

[*To face page* 96.

was, and where he was going; so he told him that it was to seek his fortune.

"Well, when you get to the place where you find it, will you think of me, and enquire the reason why my Palace is constantly falling down?"

This the Zemindar promised to do, and then continued on his journey.

The next place he arrived at was a river, and a turtle was on its bank. It asked him whither he was going, and he said: "To seek my fortune."

"Friend, remember me when it is found, and say that the poor turtle, although it lives in water, suffers from a severe burning sensation inwardly. Pray enquire the reason of this."

So the Zemindar promised, and, as a reward, the turtle bore him across the river on its back.

After another long journey, when he was both hungry and footsore, the Zemindar spied in the distance a most beautiful plum tree. It was the season for plums, so he determined to have a good feast of the fruit, and plucked one of the largest and best, but it tasted so bitter that he quickly threw it away, and, turning to the tree in anger and disappointment, cursed it.

"You are fair to look at, but otherwise good for nothing," he cried bitterly.

"Alas!" replied the tree, "this is what all travellers say to me. Yet I cannot discover why my fruits are bitter. Will you, O traveller, find out for me in your travels, and bring me word?"

After leaving the plum tree, the Zemindar went into a thick jungle, and in the midst of it found an old Fakir fast asleep. He did not know that this holy man had slept for twelve years, and was just about to awake. While he stood there the old Fakir opened his eyes, and saw him.

"Son, you have looked after me while I was asleep; who are you and where are you going?"

"I am going to seek my fortune, for I am a poor man."

"Go no further, but return the same way that you have come," said the old Fakir.

"Before I go, will you tell me, O holy Fakir, why a certain Rajah's house is always falling down, though he is constantly rebuilding it."

"The Rajah has a daughter who is grown up but unmarried; when she is married the trouble will cease."

"A turtle is troubled with burning sensations inwardly, and would be glad to know the cause."

"The turtle is full of wisdom, but selfishly keeps all its knowledge to itself. Let it tell half it knows to another, and it will become quite well."

"There is a beautiful plum tree whose fruits are bitter to the taste. What is the cause of this?"

"There is hidden treasure at the root of the tree, and when this is removed, the fruit will be sweet," said the old Fakir.

Then the Zemindar thanked him, made a low salaam, and returned the same way he had come.

First he met the plum tree, and it at once enquired if he had found out why its fruit was bitter, and he told it the reason.

"It is yours to remove that cause, my friend, so dig quickly, and see what there is at my roots."

The Zemindar did as he was bid, and found a box full of treasure—pearls, and gold, and rubies—so he tied them in his blanket, and went on his way.

At the river his friend the turtle awaited him eagerly; so the Zemindar explained everything, and the turtle said: "I will impart half the knowledge to you as a reward; stoop down and listen."

The man did as he was bid, and the creature imparted great wisdom to him in whispers.

After this he met the King, who said: "Well, traveller, what news? Have you found your fortune?"

"Yes, O King, and the cause of your trouble is, that, until your daughter is married, your house will continue to fall down."

"Will you marry her?" said the King.

The Zemindar gladly consented, and the marriage took place with great pomp. After it he returned to his own home, and there his elder brother met him.

"You see, brother," said the Zemindar, "that you said it was my fate to have but a seer of atta (flour a day), but I have found my good fortune at last."

THREE WISE MEN AND THE KING'S DAUGHTER

A KING had a very beautiful daughter, and was anxious that she should marry some one who had made himself famous in some particular way.

Three men in the city came forward and begged the King for her hand in marriage.

"But what can you do?" asked the King.

"I can tell if a thing is lost, where to find it," said the first, "and produce it if required."

The second said: "I can make such wonderful horses out of wood, that they can rise to any height and go anywhere."

The third said: "I can shoot with my bow any living thing."

The King was pleased, and went and told his daughter, asking her to choose which she would have as a husband.

"I will tell you to-morrow," said the girl.

The King agreed, but on the morrow she was nowhere to be found, and her father, much distressed, went to the three wise men.

"Now," said he to the first, "tell me where my daughter is."

"She is with the fairies," he replied, "and unless the one in charge of her is killed, she cannot return."

Then the King turned to the other two men. To the horse-maker he said: "Go and make me a horse," and to the other: "Take your bow and arrow, mount the horse, and go and shoot the fairy: bring my daughter back with you."

Forthwith the men prepared: the horse was made, and mounted by the man with his bow and arrows, then they all disappeared into the skies. There they found the King's daughter guarded by a fairy.

The third man soon shot the fairy with his bow and arrow, and, lifting the Princess upon his horse, returned with her to her father.

Now each man felt that he had an equal claim upon her, and had earned her as his wife; so the King asked her to decide.

"I will marry the man who shot the fairy," said she, "and no other."

This decision being final, they had a grand feast in celebration of her marriage.

Moral.—Those who think they have the best claim, do not always attain their desires!

BARBIL'S SON

A Rajah's son once went to worship at a sacred stone; when there, he beheld a lovely young girl, so, falling on his face before the stone, he said: "If you will but give me this girl as my bride, I will give you my head as a sacrifice."

His prayer was granted, and he married the girl.

For two months he was so happy that he never remembered his vow, but at the end of that time, a Brahmin came and reminded him of it. So, after bidding his wife a loving farewell, he went sadly away, and, *cutting off his head,* placed it near the stone as a sacrifice.

Now his father, Barbil, missing him, came there to search, and was horrified to find his son's dead body with the head offered to the stone.

"What is my life worth to me now? I will also sacrifice myself," said he, and forthwith he too cut off his own head and placed it beside that of his son.

The bride, finding neither father nor husband return, went forth in search of them; and, seeing what had happened, determined to add her own life to the sacrifice.

She was just about to destroy herself when a voice near by said: "Daughter, do not hurt yourself. The heads alone are off, but if you take them and place them beside the bodies, they will unite again."

The delighted girl immediately did as she was directed, and the two heads were united to the bodies, so that she once again saw her husband and father alive.

But no sooner did they begin to speak than she found that she had made a terrible mistake, for, in her eagerness to restore the heads to their bodies again, she had not noticed that she had united her husband's head to his father's body, and Barbil's head to her husband's body.

While the two men quarrelled over this mistake, the poor girl, greatly distressed, appealed to the Gods to help her. They bade her cease weeping.

"The head is the principal thing," said

they; "do not mind the body: if you were the daughter of a poor man and married a Prince, Barbil, having taken the form of the Prince, is also of royal blood, so it matters not. Let him that has the head of your husband be your husband again, and he who has the head of the King be the King."

Thus they settled the matter, and returned home.

Moral.—The head ruleth the body, and not the body the head!

THE TIGER AND THE RATS

An old tiger became ill in the jungles, and, being unable to use his teeth, was much troubled by rats, who used to come and eat his food before he had time to touch it.

Nearly starved to death, he appealed to the fox, who said: "Why do you not keep a cat? you will then soon be rid of your trouble."

The tiger thought this an excellent idea, and immediately sent for a cat.

Now the cat was a very cunning animal, and thought to herself, how nice it was to be in the service of the tiger. "But," said she, "I will only drive away the rats, because, if I kill them, the tiger will have no further need of me, and my employment will be gone."

So she kept watching by the tiger all night and drove away the rats.

One day she said to the tiger: "To-night,

if you do not mind, I'd like to take a holiday, and would like you to take care of my kitten."

"Very well," said the tiger.

So the cat brought the kitten, and, leaving it with the tiger, went away.

The kitten was a splendid ratter, and, not knowing why it had been put near the tiger, was surprised and delighted to see the rats, which it speedily killed; and then arranged in a line to show its mother on her return in the morning.

But as soon as the cat saw them she grew very angry, and said: "What have you done? you have taken away my employment."

The poor little kitten said that it did not know that it was not to kill rats, and was very unhappy.

Then the tiger came forward, and dismissed them both, saying: "I am now rid of the rats, and require your service no longer."

So they went away crestfallen.

Moral.—Thus do people often make a convenience of those who are their best friends!

THE ADVENTURES OF A BIRD

A SMALL bird was once half buried in a puddle and could not escape, so it called to a passing stranger for help.

"Take me out, O stranger, and as a reward, you may eat me when my feathers are dried."

So the man assisted it; but no sooner were its wings free than it flew away without expressing a word of gratitude.

After going a short distance it found a *cowrie* (or small shell, the smallest current coin in India, and now very rarely used), and joyously exclaimed: "I have found a *cowrie*, I have money—I am now higher than a Rajah."

A Rajah hearing this, sent a man to take away the *cowrie*. "See," said he, "that bird says it is higher than a Rajah."

So he took the *cowrie*, and brought it to the Rajah.

Whereupon the bird said: "See, that Rajah was *hungry*, so he took away my money."

This annoyed the Rajah so much (as only the poorest people deal in *cowries*) that he immediately restored it to the bird, who, nothing daunted, replied: "See, the Rajah was afraid, and so he has returned my *cowrie*."

This was going a little too far, and the Rajah, in a rage, ordered the offender to be shot.

Moral.—Let Well alone.

THE LEGEND OF NALDERA TEMPLE

At a little distance beyond Mushobra in the Simla district, stands an old, old temple of the Mongolian type, around which hangs a quaint wooden fringe, which causes a strange rattling sound on a windy day.

No priest lives within its sacred precincts, and the vicinity being the Viceroy's summer camping ground, the presiding "Deo," or deity, must often be disturbed by the light laughter and chatter of picnic parties from Simla.

Many years ago, before the present Rickshaw Road existed, a party of hillmen, gaily laughing and talking as they swung along, carrying a "Dandy" (or kind of litter), arrived at the place.

It was about 11 A.M. on a bright October morning, and the keen wit of the men as they exchanged repartee with many bright-eyed *Paharee* maidens, seemed in keeping with the cool, crisp air and turquoise blue sky; but suddenly a deep silence fell upon them.

They had come within sight of a number of enormous boulders which lay scattered, as though hurled by some earthquake or invisible force along the precipitous mountain side.

Not a word escaped the lips of the four men till they had turned the corner which bounds Naldera Temple; then they took out their *cheelums* and smoked while they told this tale:

"Years and years ago there stood in this place a beautiful and prosperous city, full of houses and people.

"The present Temple stood in its midst, but the people were wicked and sinful, so one day the 'Deo' arose in great wrath and hurled the entire city with its inhabitants down into the precipice, so that not one stone was left standing upon another; and the grey rocks and solitary Temple alone remain to tell the tale of past splendour and prosperity."

THE BUNNIAH'S WIFE AND THE THIEF

A BUNNIAH, or merchant, lying awake one night, saw a thief enter the room. So he whispered to his wife: "Wife, wife, a thief is in the room; what are we to do?"

Now his wife was a very clever woman, and she replied: "Why are you waking me? I was having such a fine dream."

"What did you dream?" asked her husband.

"I dreamt that I had three fine sons, and they were named 'Mugwani,' 'Hajee,' and 'Chor.'" (The last name means "thief.")

"What silly names!" said the Bunniah. "How could you call out to them?"

"By their names, of course," replied she.

"But how could you call 'Chor'? If it happened to be night, what would people think?"

"Why, I would call him like this, loud: 'Chor!' 'Chor!'" and she jumped up and ran out of the room, followed by her husband, the two calling "Chor! Chor!" as loudly as they could.

The thief, thinking they were only pretending, remained silent under the bed, waiting for their return. They soon came back with a number of friends, who caught the thief and took him away to prison.

WHO STOLE THE RUBY?

A DYING King called his three sons to him and gave each of them a ruby. "Keep this," said he, "in remembrance of your father."

The three rubies were put into a box and locked up. Some time afterwards, on opening the box, only two rubies were found in it, and the third one was missing.

Now the three sons knew that had a thief been there, he would have helped himself to all the stones, so they said within themselves: "One of our friends has done this; let us go and tell the Priest."

So they started off together, and on the way met a man, who said: "Friends, have you seen my camel?"

"Was it blind?" asked the eldest brother.

"Yes," said the man.

"Had it no tail?" asked the second.

"You are right," said the man.

"Was it carrying vinegar?" enquired the third.

"Yes," replied the man. "Did you see it?"

"No," said the brothers; "we did not see it."

"Very strange," returned the man; "you know all about it, and yet you did not see it. I will also go to the Priest and tell him about you."

So they went, and the man told the Priest his story.

"How is it that you three know all about the camel, and yet you did not see it?" said the Priest.

"Well," said the eldest, "I noticed that all the plants and shrubs on the way were eaten on one side only, so I concluded that the animal who had eaten them must have been blind not to see the other side."

"How did you know that it had no tail?"

"I saw the patch of mud where it sat down," replied the second brother, "and there was an imprint of a body but no tail."

The Priest then asked the third boy how he knew that the camel carried vinegar.

"Because all along the road were wet patches which smelt of vinegar."

These answers pleased the Priest very much, and he gave a feast for the brothers.

During the feast he sat down, and, unknown

to them, watched and listened to find out what they were talking about.

The eldest said: "This grain he has given us to eat was grown in a cemetery."

The second said: "And this meat is not killed meat; it is some other flesh."

The youngest said: "The Priest himself is a villain."

Then the Priest ran out and caught the man who had sold him the grain.

"Tell me at once where you gathered this grain?" demanded he.

"From a cemetery," confessed the man.

After this the Priest sought the butcher, and said: "Where did you get that meat you sold me? Did you kill the sheep?"

The butcher admitted that it was the flesh of a goat which had dropped dead, and had not been killed.

Going back, the Priest resolved to catch the boys in their own net, and he told them a story about two men and a thief.

"Now," said he, when he had finished, "which of the three do you prefer?"

The eldest boy said he liked one man, and the second the other, but the third preferred the thief!

"Well," said the Priest, "if you prefer the thief, you yourself must be a thief. Where is the third ruby?"

On this the boy confessed that he had stolen it; and, taking it out of his pocket, restored it to his brother. The three went home together, and lived happily ever afterwards.

THE STORY OF VICKRAMADIT

A King once asked his daughters to tell him the reason why they were so comfortable and always clothed in fine raiment, with jewels to wear, and a Palace to live in.

They all said: "It is because we are your daughters, O King!"

But the youngest said: "I am what I am through my favourable destiny, and not because I happen to be your daughter; if good fortune be destined for us we shall have it under any circumstances."

At this the King was very angry, and said: "Leave my Palace at once, and see what your own luck will do for you; methinks your lucky stars will cease to shine once you have left my Palace."

But in order to further humiliate her, he determined to get her married to the poorest man in his kingdom, and one who was weak and sickly and about to die.

He therefore sent his servants to bring the first sickly-looking pauper they could find.

Now it so happened about this time that one Vickramadit, a holy mendicant, was lying outside the Palace gates stricken down with great suffering, and almost at the point of death; and they brought him as the most suitable man for the young Princess to marry.

The poor beggar Vickramadit was in reality a great King, who once reigned over the ancient and holy city of Ujjain; but he had abdicated his throne in order to become a "Sanyasi," or begging Fakir, and was then on a pilgrimage to Kasi, the holy city of Benares, where he hoped to pass the rest of his days in prayer, and the deeds of charity for which he was well known.

The sickness with which he was stricken down at the gates of the King's Palace was caused through his great love of God's creatures, and happened in this way.

One day, as he was walking along footsore and tired, a snake came up to him and said: "Can you give me some water to drink, for I am dying of thirst?"

Vickramadit replied: "I have no water in

my gourd, having just drank it; but if you will promise not to harm me, you may creep down my throat into my body, and there drink your fill and return satisfied."

This the snake promised, but, instead of returning, it remained within him and refused to come back.

All that the beggar ate passed into the mouth of the snake; and in this way he soon found himself unable to travel, and obliged to rest, suffering at the same time great agonies from starvation and thirst.

When the King's servants found and brought him to the Palace, the young Princess was there and then forced to marry Vickramadit, and expelled from the town with her beggar husband.

Both King and Queen expressed a hope at parting that she would soon learn the lesson, that it was all due to them alone that she had fared so well hitherto.

As Vickramadit could not travel very far owing to weakness, she took shelter in the first small hut she could find, and there stayed, trying to alleviate his sufferings.

Now, near this hut was a mound of earth in which dwelt a snake. In the evenings, as is usual in India, the snake came out of his hole and stood on the mound of earth, where he hissed violently.

The snake which lived inside Vickramadit heard the sound, and hissed in reply. Then they began a conversation.

The snake on the mound said: "You traitor! You were given permission to drink water; and this is how you treat the holy Fakir, and break your promise to return without doing him any harm! You shall now be given a certain seed to eat which will entirely destroy your body, and you will die in agonies."

The other snake replied: "You miser! You 'dog in the manger,' who live over a mound beneath which lies vast treasures and priceless jewels! You know that you cannot use them yourself, and yet you will allow nobody else to touch them! Your end will be that a woman will kill you by pouring boiling milk and butter over you."

The young wife heard these two snakes denouncing each other, and determined to act upon what she had overheard. When leaving her father's house, she had managed to hide on her person a small pearl ring, and this she now pawned for a small sum of money, and purchased milk and butter.

Warming these to boiling point, she went over at midday and poured them into the snake's hole in the mound.

She also sought the seed, which would kill the snake her husband had swallowed, and gave it to him to eat.

Thus both snakes were killed, and all danger from them ceased to exist.

Vickramadit, after the destruction of the snake, improved rapidly, and soon regained his health and strength.

The young wife now turned her attention to the mound of earth, beneath which lay buried treasures.

She employed a few men to dig, and they soon unearthed several *ghurras*, or earthen vessels, full of priceless gems.

With these she went away, and very soon founded a great city, over which she made her lord King.

Thus Vickramadit once more reigned a King; and no Queen was more famous than the young Princess who had been so cruelly cast adrift by her father.

The old father heard of this new King,

and of all the riches and splendour of his Court and Queen; and he sent men to enquire if it were true that his daughter was really as great as people reported.

The men returned and said: "O King, her riches, the magnificence of her Court and Palace, surpass all we have heard; she is indeed a great Queen, and has founded a mighty city."

The King then owned his mistake, and said: "My daughter was right when she said her greatness was due more to her individual luck than to the mere fact that she happened to be born my daughter; for has she not, in spite of all my ill-treatment of her, risen to be Queen, not of a small kingdom such as mine, but of a world-renowned kingdom."

Moral.—Thy kismet is thy fate; when that is good, then the most unfavourable circumstances, or the deepest gloom, cannot prevent its asserting itself.

THE WEAVER

THERE was a weaver who was unmarried, and all that he could earn in a day, in exchange for the cloth he wove, only amounted to two pounds of either rice or other grain.

One day he cooked some *kitcherie*,[1] and, placing it in a plate, left it to get cool, and went out to sell his cloth.

While he was away a jackal came and ate up the *kitcherie*; and on his return he found the jackal, so he tied it up and beat it severely.

Then he cooked some bread, which he ate, and again beat the jackal.

The poor creature thought: "Now my life will go, if this man keeps on beating me in this way."

When the man next went out to dispose of his cloth, the jackal, tied up by itself,

[1] A dish made of rice and lentils cooked together with clarified butter or *ghee*, and then boiled.

felt very lonely, especially as it could hear its companions howling in the jungles; so it began to howl too, and, hearing it, one of its friends came to see where it was, and finding it, said: "Brother, what are you doing here?"

The poor jackal, bruised all over and swollen with the beating it had received, replied: "Friend, a man has caught me, and takes the greatest care of me; see how fat I have grown with eating all the *hulwa-poories*[1] he gives me. If you will release me, I will tie you here, and you will get a share of the good things."

So the two exchanged places, and the first jackal ran back gladly into the jungles.

On the return of the weaver he, as usual, began to beat the poor creature, who then spoke, and said: "Why are you beating me?"

The weaver, surprised, replied: "I have never heard this jackal speak before!"

"That one has gone, and he tied me here in his place, and told me I should get all sorts of good things to eat; but if you will release me, I will arrange a marriage with a King's daughter for you."

[1] Another native dainty made with sugar, etc.

"What!" said the man, "I am only a poor weaver, and can you really get me married to a King's daughter?"

"Yes," returned the jackal.

So the weaver released it, and turning itself into a Brahmin, it crossed the river and presented itself at the court of a certain Rajah, to whom it said: "O King, I have found a rich weaver-caste Rajah, who wishes your daughter's hand in marriage."

The Rajah, much pleased, consented, and the Brahmin, on getting outside the Palace, once more turned into a jackal, and returned to the weaver.

"Follow me," said he, "and I will take you to the King's daughter."

So the weaver took up his blanket, which was all he possessed.

On their way they met a Dhobie, or washerman, carrying his bundle of clothes. The jackal gave him a gold mohur, and told him to spread all the clean clothes he possessed upon the trees around.

Further on they met a cotton-beater, or man who, in the East, beats cotton and prepares it to make up into pillows and quilts; to him they also gave a gold mohur, and asked in return for several large balls of cotton.

These they carried on a large plate to the river; and the jackal, leaving the weaver, returned as a Brahmin to the Rajah, who had seen the Dhobie's clothes in the distance, and thought they were tents pitched by his daughter's future husband.

The jackal had told the weaver to watch, and, as soon as he saw him enter the Palace, he was to take large lumps of cotton and throw them one by one into the river, so that they might be seen floating down the stream.

"The Bridegroom," explained the Brahmin, "has met with a terrible accident; all his possessions and his followers are lost in the river, and only he and I remain, dressed in the clothes in which we stand."

Then the Rajah ordered his musicians and followers to come out, and go with horses in great pomp to bring the weaver, who was forthwith married to the Princess.

After the marriage the Brahmin said: "This son-in-law of yours has lost all he had; what is the use of his returning to his country? Let him stay here with you."

To this the Rajah, who loved his daughter, gladly consented, and gave them a fine house and grounds.

Now the weaver, who was not accustomed to good society, or to living with those above his station in life, made a *salaam*, or obeisance, such as a poor man is wont to do, to his wife every morning, and she began to suspect that he had deceived her, and was not a real Rajah. So she asked him one day to tell her the whole truth about himself, and he did so.

"Well," said she, "you have owned it to me, but do not let my father or mother know; for now that I am married to you, things cannot be altered, and it is better that they should remain in ignorance; but whatever my father may ask you to do, promise me that you will do it, always answering 'Yes, I will,' to anything he may suggest."

To this the weaver agreed; and shortly afterwards the Rajah called him and enquired if he was willing to help him, and, as promised, the man replied, "Yes, I will." Then he went to his wife and told her, and she commended him.

Next day the King told him that two

brothers, by name "Darya" and "Barjo," threatened to fight and take his kingdom from him, and he desired his son-in-law to go to the stables and select a horse on which to ride on the morrow to battle.

In the stables was a horse that was standing on three legs. "This," thought the weaver, "will just suit me, for it seems lame and has only three legs to go on, and making this an excuse, I'll keep behind all the rest, and out of danger."

Now this horse[1] used to eat a quarter of a pound of opium daily, and could fly through the air, so that when the Rajah heard of the selection he was very delighted, and said to himself: "What a clever man this is, that he is able to discover which is the best horse!"

The day following he had the horse brought round, and mounted it in fear and trembling, having himself securely tied on lest he should fall off, while, to weight himself equally, he fastened a small millstone on either side.

As soon as the groom released the horse, it flew up into the air, then down again, and

[1] This is a well-directed piece of sarcasm against native horse-dealers who drug their horses; also against would-be judges of horse-flesh.

then up through the branches of trees, which broke off and clung to the weaver's arms and body, so that he presented a strange spectacle. He was terrified, and kept on crying out: "O Darya! Barjo! for your sakes have I come to my death."

The two Princes, Darya and Barjo, seeing this strange horse flying through the air, and hearing their names coming from a queer object all covered with branches of trees, were very much alarmed, and said: "If more come like this, we shall indeed be lost; *one* is enough for us."

So they wrote to the King, and said: "We have seen your warrior; stay in your country, and we will stay in ours: we cannot fight."

And they sent him a peace-offering.

THE DOG WHO WAS A RAJAH

A DAUGHTER was once born to a Brahmin and his wife, and from the day of its birth a dog came daily and laid down in the house.

This made the mother say, in jest, when the child would not cease crying: "Stop, or I shall give you to the dog."

And the Brahmin added: "I will give her to the dog when she is grown up."

When the girl grew up, he said to the dog one day, in a fit of temper: "Here, take my daughter, and do as you wish with her."

The mother now regretted her jest, which had suggested this idea to her husband, and said: "Here, my child, take this handful of seeds, and, as you go, strew them along the road, so that I may know where to find you."

As the girl went along she scattered the seeds, and at last she arrived at a field in which was a small *baoli*, or well. Here she sat down, and told the dog she was thirsty.

"Go and drink from the well," said the dog.

As she approached the dog followed her, and they saw a ladder leading to the bottom of the well, so that they climbed down and came to a fine house with lovely gardens and flowers, and servants ready to receive them. These belonged to the dog, who was in reality a Rajah, and only assumed the shape of a dog when he left the well.

Some time after this the Brahmin expressed a wish to go and visit his daughter. So his wife told him to follow the track of any freshly sprung-up little plants he might see.

He followed out her directions, and found the small trees led to the well; and as he felt thirsty, he looked in and saw the ladder; so he descended by it, and found the dog had become a Rajah.

Going round the grounds with his daughter, he noticed a house made of gold. "What is this?" asked he.

"It is for you, my father."

So he went in and found everything perfect, except that in one of the walls was a great crack.

"That crack," explained the Rajah, who had joined them, "was caused when you first drank water at the well; and it will remain there until you undo the wrong you did your daughter in giving her to a dog, for you did not then know who he really was. To undo the wrong you must serve me as my cowherd for twelve years, after which time the crack in the wall will close up of its own accord."

The Brahmin then went to his wife and told her all that had happened; and they returned together to the Rajah, whose cows he tended for twelve years, after which the crack in the golden wall came together of itself; and thus the wrong was righted.

THE FOURTH WIFE IS THE WISEST

THERE was a Bunniah who had an only son, who had married four wives; of these, three were fools, and only one was wise.

For some reason the Rajah of that country got angry with the Bunniah, and said that he and all his family were to go away, for he would not permit them to remain in his kingdom any longer; also, they were not to take away any of their jewels or possessions with them, except such things as they were wearing at the time.

Hearing this, the youngest of the four wives asked if she might be allowed to bake some bread, to take for them to eat on the journey.

This was permitted, and, in kneading the flour, she dropped four very valuable and beautiful rubies into it, and then having cooked the bread, showed it to the people as she left, and said: "See, I take nothing with me except this bread."

They journeyed far away into another country, and were very poor. Then the Bunniah said to his youngest daughter-in-law: "Daughter, what are we to do to live? We have no money and no clothes."

She was silent for a long time, and then said: "We must sell our jewels, but in the meantime take this"—giving him one of the rubies—"and sell it."

Now this ruby was worth a very great deal of money, and the Bunniah took it gratefully, thinking all the time what a wise girl his daughter-in-law was, to think of bringing it as she had done.

He then went to a rich merchant, who in reality was not a merchant at all, but a clever thief, and who, as soon as he set eyes on the ruby, knew it to be a valuable one, and determined to have it.

"Go," said he to one of his servants, "and bring me a basket full of money that I may pay for this valuable stone;" and as the servant left, he turned to the Bunniah, offering him a chair, and said: "Sit down, friend."

Now this chair was a specially prepared one, being kept by the thief as a trap for the unwary. The seat was of raw cotton, under which was a great hole into which anybody who sat on the chair would fall. It was carefully covered over with a piece of clean white cloth, so that nothing was noticed.

On it the poor Bunniah sat, and as the soft cotton gave way under him, he found himself in the hole, over which the thief carefully placed a great stone and left him, while he quietly pocketed the ruby.

As the Bunniah did not return to his home for many days, his daughter-in-law called her husband, and gave him the second ruby. "Go, seek thy father," said she; "and if you find him, bring me back this ruby, and buy food and clothes with one you will find with him."

The young man searched high and low for his father, but, not finding him, he decided to sell his ruby, and by ill chance went to the same merchant who had robbed the Bunniah.

The thief treated him in exactly the same way, and, after having stolen the ruby, trapped him into the same hole as his father.

Finding that neither husband nor father returned, the woman sold her jewels, and bought clothes and food for the rest of the family; but for herself she secretly bought the outfit of a policeman, or *chowkidar*, and resolved to work in that capacity. So she presented herself at the King's Court, and he, taking a fancy to the handsome face of the young man (for she was disguised as such), gave her employment.

Living in the jungles near that place was a terrible "Rakhas," or evil spirit, and that night, while on duty, the new policeman was startled by a roar like that of a tiger; but as soon as the "Rakhas" perceived him, it assumed the form of a woman, and coming up, said weeping: "The Rajah has hanged my husband, and I wish to see him once more, but cannot reach because the gallows are high."

"Climb upon my back," said the policeman.

The woman did so, but as soon as she got near enough she began to eat her supposed husband.

On this the young policeman, drawing his sword, cut off the woman's head, and as she fell, being enchanted, she disappeared, but a silver anklet from one of her feet was left behind.

Next morning the policeman carried the anklet to the King, and told him what had happened, and how the strange woman had disappeared as he struck her with his sword.

The King was much pleased at the youth's bravery, and also with the silver anklet, which was full of precious stones of great value, and, turning to the policeman, he said: "Ask what you will, and I will give it to you, even if you ask my daughter in marriage."

The man replied: "O King, I ask nothing; but grant me, I pray you, control over the entire bazaar, that I may kill, banish, hang, or release, and do as I like with the people who dwell there."

The King granted this request, and having discovered the thief in the supposed merchant, the policeman went to him and boldly demanded the release of his father and son.

But the thief denied all knowledge of the affair.

Then the young man entered the shop, and, lifting up the great stone, beheld the two unfortunate men, who were nearly starved to death.

Having released them, he took the thief to the King, and told him what had happened. After they had hanged the wicked thief, the young policeman changed his clothes and appeared as a woman.

The King was greatly surprised, but so pleased at all she had done, that he called her his "daughter," and gave her husband, father, and other relations money and goods, so that they lived in contentment for the rest of their lives.

THE STORY OF PIR SAB

VERY, very far away in the north of India is a big river, and many years ago there lived, not very far from its banks, an old woman who had an only daughter—a beautiful girl, who, when she grew up, was given in marriage to a man who lived in a village on the opposite bank of the river; and all preliminaries being arranged, a day was fixed for the marriage party with the bride to cross over.

A gay company with songs and music set out, and everything went well until they reached the middle of the stream. The current is strong and dangerous in that place, and in less time than it takes to say it, the joyous party, with its music and songs and drummers, and the litter which held the bride, was hurled into the seething water, and every soul sank and was drowned.

The old woman alone, who had remained

at home on account of her feeble age, escaped, and sad indeed was she when she came to hear of her daughter's fate.

Her own home grew lonely and uncongenial to her, so, in a half-frenzied state, she betook herself to the river side, and there spent many hours every day calling to the river to give up her dead.

This went on for twenty years! One day Pir Sab, a pious Mahamedan, arrived there, and was about to say his prayers when the old woman attracted his attention.

"Pray, why do you weep, old woman?" he said.

"For my child, a beautiful bride who, with all her wedding guests, was drowned in this river twenty years ago."

"Twenty years! and you have mourned so long?" Thus saying, Pir Sab dismounted from his horse, and covering his head with a sheet, he stood by the river and cried: "O river, restore the dead! O river, restore the dead! O river, restore the dead!"

At the third cry a bridal party was seen to approach, and the long-lost ones, with the young bride, were restored to the old woman as unchanged as upon the day they were

THE STORY OF PIR SAB

The old woman alone remained at home on account of her feeble age.

[*To face page* 142.

drowned, and in perfect ignorance of the flight of years.

A voice was then heard from the Great Unseen, which said: "O Pir Sab, I have heard your prayer. At your first cry these restored ones came forth from the fishes, who had eaten them; at your second call I re-formed them into human form; and at your third call they went forth with life."

Now, who was Pir Sab, and how did he possess this power?

Mahamed, when he was upon earth, sometimes took flights into Heaven. On such occasions he generally called on anybody near at hand to assist him up, or give him a push upwards. On one occasion he had called thrice for help without meeting with any response, when Pir Sab, a strong man, knelt before him, and with one spring from his shoulder, Mahamed reached the fourth Heavens!

In return for this kindness it was granted to Pir Sab to perform miracles.

Note.—The man who related this story to me added the following modern miracle:

"During the late Chitral expedition there was with Umra Khan's forces a remarkable man, the son of one

Akhum Sab, who died some years ago. Now Akhum Sab was a devout man, who never failed to pray every Friday, as all good Mahamedans do, with their faces turned towards Mecca, the holy city, which is four months' journey from the north of India, so that many who wish to visit it cannot. Yet this man used to enter his room, and close the door at two o'clock daily, and come out *after seven minutes* (you may believe me or not); but, during those seven minutes, he *went to Mecca, said his prayers in the holy Mosque there*, and returned! This he did every Friday; I have seen it with my own eyes!"
—A.E.D.

THE ORIGIN OF A RIVER

THERE stands on the old Agra Bombay Road, between Goona in Central India and Jhansi, a small village beside a stream, and this used to be a bathing stage for travellers in the old days, before railways were known in India.

In the village there once lived a man whose wife died, leaving an only daughter. The girl, as she grew to womanhood, had a very bad time of it, as all the housework fell upon her shoulders. She had to cook her father's food and carry it to him in the fields; to draw water for the cattle and look after them, besides many other things which took up her time and strength.

So she invoked the aid of the Gods.

Next time she went to draw water from the well, which was a very deep one, and required a long, long string for the bucket, she looked in, and lo! the water had risen to the top, and was almost overflowing, so that there was no need to draw any; and her father's cattle stood round and drank their fill.

Then she filled her *chattie* with water, and enjoyed a bath in the sunshine.

After a time the water sank to its usual level. Thus far all was well, but her father noticed how quickly the cattle had been watered, and how soon his daughter returned home: also he missed the long rope which she always carried on her arm. He began to suspect that some unknown man, a stranger to himself, used to help her, and determined to watch.

A great fig tree grew beside the well; and one day he concealed himself in its branches.

As usual, his daughter came with the cattle, and all happened as before. He was struck with wonder and amazement at what he saw.

Just as the girl was about to take her usual bath, she looked up and saw him.

In a moment she felt that he had suspected her of some evil. "Father," cried she, "why do you look with an evil eye on your child? Do you not believe that the Gods have helped her?"

But before her father could reply, she sank down to the bottom of the well with the water and never rose again, for the outraged Gods took her to themselves; and, in token of their displeasure, the well was cleft from top to bottom, and hillocks formed on either side. From this spot flows a tiny stream, which, if you follow it, becomes a mighty river.

THE GOLDEN SCORPIONS

THERE once lived in a certain village a poor man who went out daily to beg, carrying in his hand a small vessel made from a gourd, such as the Jogis, or holy Fakirs, in India use.

In it he carried home his scanty meal of flour each evening.

One day he placed the gourd, which was empty at the time, upon the ground, and went to some little distance to drink water.

On his return he was amazed to find it full of scorpions.

Seizing it on one side, he carefully knocked it against a stone until the venomous things dropped off.

Great indeed was his surprise to find when he next looked into his gourd, that several scorpions still clung to it, but had been transformed by the Gods into pure gold, although their forms were retained.

Thus the good old man was enriched, but great was his disappointment when he remembered how many scorpions he had thrown away, for these might also have turned into gold had he kept them.

Moral.—There is good sometimes in even the evil things in life.

THE STORY OF A PEARL

A POOR workman and his wife were once almost starving. Every day the man gathered sticks and sold them, while the woman remained at home.

"Wife," said the man one day, "come, we will *both* go and gather wood for sale to-day, so that, if we earn enough, we shall not eat rice only, but will buy a small fish, and eat that also."

The woman agreed, and having sold their stock of firewood, they returned home with a fish for dinner.

On opening it, a small white bead, round and shining, fell upon the floor. The woman was attracted by its brightness, and locked it up in a box.

Many days of poverty and hunger visited that household before the woman remembered the pretty stone found in the fish; but at last she thought of it, and took it to a Bunniah, who, as soon as he set eyes upon it, said: "Give me that, and I will give you as much as you can carry away of *ghee* and food and oil, not only to-day, but for many days, if you will come to my shop."

The foolish woman parted with her treasure, not knowing that it was a pearl of great value, and returned home laden with good things.

The Bunniah chuckled with delight. He was crafty, like all Bunniahs, and, you may depend, never kept his promise: such was the foolishness of the woman, and such the cunning and greed of the man.

THE BUNNIAH'S GHOST

FAR away in a valley in the Himalayan mountains lies a little village, where once lived a good man who had his home beside a field in which grew a beautiful mulberry tree—so big and so beautiful that it was the wonder of the country round.

Hundreds of people were wont to gather together beneath it, and the poor carried away basket loads of its fruit. Thus it became a meeting place where a *mela*, or fair, was held when the fruit season was on.

Now the fame of it reached a certain Rajah who had rented out the land, and one day he came with all his retinue to see it.

"There is no such tree in the Royal Gardens," said the Grand Vizier.

"It is not meet that a subject should possess what the Rajah hath not," added the Prime Minister.

The Rajah replied not a word, for his heart

THE BUNNIAH'S GHOST

Could it be fancy, or did he see a strange man standing before him?

[*To face page* 152.

was filled with envy; and that night, before going to bed, he gave orders that, on a certain day, in the early dawn, before anybody was astir, a party of armed men should take their axes to the village, and fell the mulberry tree even with the ground. But ill dreams disturbed the Rajah's rest, and he could not sleep.

Could it be fancy, or did he really see a strange man standing before him?

The strange man spoke: "O King, live for ever! I am the spirit of a Bunniah (or merchant) who died in yonder village many years ago. During my lifetime I defrauded the people. I gave them short measure and adulterated their food.

"When I died and passed into the Land of Unhappy Spirits, the Gods, who are just, O King! decreed that I should give back what I had stolen. My soul therefore went into a mulberry tree, where year after year the people gather fruit, and regain their losses.

"In one year more they will be repaid to the uttermost *cowrie*;[1] but you mean to destroy the tree and drive my soul I know not whither. Wherefore have I come to

[1] The smallest current or *shell* money of India.

plead with you to spare it this once, for when a year is past it will die of itself and my soul find its way to that Land of Shadows which is the abode of the Gods—where it will find peace."

So the Rajah listened, and the strange man went away.

For one year longer the people sat as before under the cool shadow of the mulberry tree, and then it died. And was that all?

No: when they cut it down there was found deep in the earth *one* living root, and that they left, for who can destroy the soul?

Hindu Proverb.—"*Pün ki jar sada hari.*" (The roots of charity are always green.)

BICKERMANJI THE INQUISITIVE

THERE was a certain Rajah whose name was Bickermanji. He was very inquisitive, and always wished to know everything that was going on in his kingdom, and what his subjects were doing.

At night he disguised himself in common clothes and a blanket, and walked quietly in the streets and bazaars to spy on the people. Next day, when complaints were brought to him of the doings of this or that person, he knew all about it.

In this way he observed that a certain woman, the wife of a Sowcar, or Bunniah, used to leave her home every night, carrying a *ghurra,* or *chattie,* on her head and some food in her hand. Arrived at the river, she floated the *chattie,* and sat upon it, thus getting a passage to the other side, where she visited a certain Fakir.

In the early morning she returned, carrying

the *chattie* full of water for the day's use; and this being an everyday custom with native women in the East, it was never suspected that she had spent nearly the whole night away from her home. Bickermanji observed all this, and wondered to himself how the matter would end.

One day the woman's husband, who had been away in another country, returned, so she had to attend to his food, and could not get away as early as usual to carry dainty dishes to the Fakir, who was very angry when she arrived late, and made her excuses on account of her husband's arrival.

"What do I care for your husband?" said the Fakir. "Is he better than a holy mendicant? Go this moment and bring me his head."

This she did, much to the Fakir's surprise; but, instead of being pleased at her obedience to his wishes, he was angry, and said: "If you killed your husband, you will one day kill me also."

So he drove her from his presence, and she returned to her own home, where, taking her husband's head upon her knee, she set up a great weeping and lamentation, which attracted all her neighbours and brought them together.

"My husband had only just returned from a journey, bringing money; and see, thieves have stolen his money, and murdered him during the night."

Her neighbours believed this, and prepared to carry her husband to the burning ghât, for he was a Hindoo. While they did this, the woman declared that she would follow, and perform the sacred rite of *suttee*, or being burnt upon her husband's funeral pyre.

Although impressed by her supposed devotion to her husband, her friends wrote to Bickermanji, and begged him to prevent her.

Bickermanji knew all that had really happened, and meant to show his own wisdom and the woman's crime, also to punish her as he thought best. So he promptly forbade the *suttee*.

The widow then wrote to Rajah Bickermanji's stepmother, a very clever woman, and asked her to intercede, that she might die with her husband. Then his stepmother said: "My son, allow this *suttee* to take place, and within eight days I will give you my reasons."

This aroused the curiosity of his nature, and, much against his will, he consented; so the woman had her own way.

He waited impatiently for the eight days to be over, and then went to his stepmother, who ordered a dooly, and, taking with her a goat, asked him to accompany her to the nearest temple. Arrived there, she asked him to stand at the door, and left the goat outside.

"If, when I come to the door, I say 'kill,' you are to kill the goat, but if not, stand where you are," were the old woman's instructions as she went to make her offering of fruit and flowers and sweets.

Soon she returned, and said: "Kill," so Bickermanji cut off the head of the goat. "Sit upon the head, my son."

And he did as he was told, but no sooner had he done so, when the head rose up into the air with him, away through space for hundreds of miles, until he came to a wall which surrounded a space twelve miles square. In this was a garden and beautiful house; and after wandering some little time, Bickermanji found water and food, a comfortable couch to lie upon, and a *hookah*, or native pipe, to smoke, but not a human being was anywhere to be seen. This puzzled him, but as he was both hungry and tired, he made a good meal, smoked his *hookah*, and laid down to sleep.

"If I sleep, I sleep, if I die, I die; a man can but die once."

Now the place belonged to a *purree*, or winged fairy being, who used to come to it during the night, and remain away all day. The servants came an hour or two beforehand just to see everything was comfortable; and when they found Bickermanji lying fast asleep, they wished to kill him, but an old woman interceded on his behalf, so they let him alone until the *purree* came.

Bickermanji was greatly surprised to see a strange winged being standing before him, and expected immediate death; but the Strange One spoke kindly, and begged him not to fear, but to make the place his home for as long as he liked.

Each day passed by quietly, and in the pleasures and ease of his present existence, Bickermanji soon forgot his kingdom, his wife, and his children.

Before going away one morning the *purree*

said: "There are four rooms in this house which you must never open; I will point them out to you, but, for the rest, you may use them as you will."

This request at once excited Bickermanji's old spirit of curiosity; and, as soon as he found himself alone, he went quickly to the door of the first room and opened it.

Within stood a horse, which turned gladly towards him, and said: "I have not seen the light of day, or had an hour's freedom, ever since I was given to the fairy by Rajah Sudra. If you will take me out, I will show you all the world, and even the secret place where the fairies dance."

Bickermanji was delighted, and immediately led out the horse, which he saddled, mounted, and rode for a wonderful and delightful ride.

In the evening the fairy, or *purree*, again warned him against opening any of the four forbidden doors; but the very next day he opened the second one, and there found a large elephant chained up.

The elephant complained bitterly of its fate, and begged Bickermanji to pity it, and take it out, which, if he did, it would in return show him much that was wonderful in the world; so Bickermanji again had a very interesting day.

On the morning following he opened the third door and found a camel inside. It too took him to all sorts of new and interesting places which were the haunts of fairy beings.

Now only one door was left, and Bickermanji determined to open that also; and when he did, he beheld a donkey, standing inside. The donkey complained just as the other animals had done, and begged for its release; but as Bickermanji mounted it for his usual ride, he found himself back in his old kingdom.

"My back aches," said the donkey; "leave me a while to rest, and go you, in the meantime, to the nearest bazaar for food. When you return you will find me here."

But when Bickermanji returned there was no donkey to be seen; so he tore his hair and wept bitterly, asking all the passers-by if any of them had seen his *ghuddee*, or donkey.

Many of the inhabitants of the town recognised him, and said: "Our Rajah has come back, and is asking for his *ghuddee*," which, in Hindustanee, means "throne" as well as "donkey."

At last his stepmother heard of his return,

and sent for him. He told her that he would give anything to be able to return to the place from which the donkey had brought him.

"Was it not I who sent you there," she replied, "and could not I send you back again? What are you willing to do in order to return? Are you willing to slay your own son to go?"

"Yes, I would even do that."

"Well, come with me as before to the temple, only, instead of a goat, take your son with you, and a sword. When I say 'kill' you must kill, but not before."

So the three went to the temple, and the stepmother stood in the doorway and cried "Kill"; but before the Rajah could raise his sword she rushed forward and seized it.

"Stop! do not kill your son. Do you remember the *suttee*, and how you judged her and wished to punish her for killing her husband on account of a friend, and now you would kill your own son for the sake of pleasure! All that has happened has been done to teach you a lesson; go you to your Palace, and there reign with greater wisdom than before."

Moral.—"Judge not, that ye be not judged."

THE BRAHMIN'S DAUGHTER

A CERTAIN Brahmin's wife had no affection for her seven stepdaughters, and persuaded their father to get rid of them. So he invited the girls to come with him on a visit to their grandmother, but on the way he slipped away quietly and left them eating plums in the jungle.

After a while they found themselves all alone, and as night fell were very frightened, and hid themselves in the hollow of a large tree. Here a tiger found them and ate six, leaving only the youngest sister alive.

She hid in the tree for several days, and at last a Rajah found her, and asked how she had got there. Then she told him the whole story, and he felt pity for her and married her.

But she often wondered what had become of her father, and whether he was alive or dead; and when she remembered the fate of her sisters, she secretly made up her mind to be revenged on her stepmother.

Then she called a crow, and asked it if it would go to her former home with a letter from her. In the letter she told her father of her sisters' fate and of her own good fortune.

The crow carried the news to her father, and, greatly surprised, he read the contents of his daughter's letter to his wife.

The woman was mercenary as well as cruel, and advised him to lose no time in visiting her, and bringing back all the money he could secure.

So the Brahmin went and spent eight or nine days in the Palace.

As he was preparing to return home, the girl called him, and gave him a box containing a snake, a scorpion, and a wasp; and as it was securely locked, he had no suspicion of its contents.

"Take this," she said, "and give it with the key to my mother; let her be alone in her room when she receives it, so that she may enjoy my gifts by herself."

Then she gave him another box full of clothes and jewels and money for himself.

After a long journey, the Brahmin arrived at his home, and said to his wife: "This box is for me, and this one for you; keep it carefully, and open it when you are alone; here is the key." So saying he went out, shut the door, and put on the chain.

Soon the woman began to cry: "I'm bitten, I'm bitten!" but he mistook it for "I've eaten, I've eaten!" meaning that he should come and share the feast. So he replied: "I've had my share, you eat what is your own share."

When he opened the door, he found her dead, so he packed up his things and returned to his daughter, and lived happily ever after.

ABUL HUSSAIN

THERE was a man called Abul Hussain who was once very rich, but had been so foolish in entertaining all his friends that he lost all his money, and became very poor.

He and his old mother lived together, and sometimes, when he felt lonely, he would walk out and call in two or three men, any passing strangers whom he chanced to meet, and ask them to come in and have a talk and smoke with him. When they left his house, he never expected to see them again.

On one occasion he accosted a man dressed in plain clothes, who, with two others, was taking a stroll, and said: "Friend, come in and have a chat with me."

The man—who was really the King—with his two followers, went in; and, after they had talked some time and made merry over wine, Abul said: "I should like to exchange places with the King for just one day."

"Why?" asked the King.

"Because the Priest who prays in the Musjid here, and his four friends, are very wicked men, and I should like to have them killed."

The King, while talking, took out some powder which had the effect of putting a person to sleep, and secretly dropped it into the wine Abul was drinking. Shortly afterwards Abul fell into a deep sleep.

The King then said to his servants: "Remove this man and take him to my Palace; change his clothes for some of mine, place him in my bed, and, until I give further orders, recognise him as your King, and let him use as much money as he likes."

The servants did as he told them, took up the sleeping man and put him to bed in the King's Palace.

Early next morning the servants came to wake Abul, and said: "Will Your Majesty rise this morning?"

Abul rubbed his eyes and looked, and behold, he was in a King's room and the King's servant was addressing him! He saw his clothes, and wondered who he was, and what had happened: then he turned to the man and said: "Who am I?"

The man replied: "You are our King."

"Am I?" returned the puzzled Abul, and, rising, he heard strains of music, and knew that the band was playing, as it always does on the awaking of a King in the morning.

He washed and dressed and went with his Vizier to hold court. While there, he said to his courtiers: "There is a man living in a certain house, and his name is Abul, I want you to take to his mother a bag of a thousand rupees. Also go to the Musjid; catch the old Priest, give him one hundred stripes, put him and his four friends on donkeys, and drive them out of the city."

All day Abul reigned as King, but when night came, the servants, who had been instructed what to do by the real King, once more put sleeping powder into his wine, and while he slept removed him to his own home, and put him into his own bed again.

When he awoke there in the morning he called to his servants, but no one answered, except his old mother, who came and stood beside him.

"Why do you call your servants?" she asked.

"Because I am a King," he replied. "Who are you?"

"I am your mother, my son, and think you must be dreaming. If the King hears about this he will be so angry that perhaps he will have you killed. You are only the son of a poor man; and do not vex the King, for he has been very good, and sent us a present of a thousand rupees yesterday."

Abul, however, would not listen, but kept on insisting that he was King, so at last the King had him locked up in prison, declaring that he must be mad. There he was kept until he ceased to say that he was King, and then he was released.

On his return home, he once more invited some strange men, and, as before, the King was amongst them, and again surreptitiously put the sleeping powder into Abul's wine, and caused him to be removed and put into his Palace on his bed while he was unconscious.

Next morning on waking Abul felt sure that it must be a dream this time, and he kept rubbing his eyes and asking the servants who he was. The servants replied: "Why, you are our King."

Abul was more than puzzled, and, pointing to his arms, which still bore the marks of bruises from stripes received in prison, said: "If I am really the King, why have I these bruises? I have been put in prison, and these are the marks where I was beaten."

But the servant said: "Your Majesty is dreaming; you are a King, and a very great King."

On this Abul got up, and hearing the strains of music, he was so delighted at his lucky position that he began to dance about the room, while the King, who was peeping from a doorway, stood and laughed so much that he was almost choked. At last, being unable to restrain himself longer, he called out: "O Abul, do you wish to kill me with laughter?"

On this Abul discovered that the King had been playing a practical joke on him, and he said: "O King, you have given me much misery."

"Have I?" said the King. "Well, as much misery as I have given you, so much pleasure shall you now have;" and he gave him a present of heaps of money and a beautiful wife, sending him away with the assurance that he would never be poor any more.

Very soon Abul ran through all his money, and, hoping to get some more from the King, planned with his wife to pay another visit to the Palace.

Then he went to the King and, crying and wringing his hands, said: "O King, my wife is dead."

The King, much shocked and grieved, gave him a *than*[1] of cloth and a thousand rupees, and told him to go and bury his wife.

In the meantime his wife had gone to the Queen's apartments, and there, throwing herself on her face, she wept and said: "O Queen, my husband is dead, and I am most unhappy!"

The Queen, deeply grieved, gave her a thousand rupees and a *than* of cloth, saying: "Go, bury thy dead."

Abul and his wife were now most happy, and set to work to make themselves clothes with the new cloth they had received.

[1] A *than* is a length of cloth which varies from five yards to twenty yards, or more.

Now it happened that day that the King went to see his Queen, and, finding her in tears, enquired the cause of her grief.

"Abul's wife has just been to say Abul is dead."

"No," said the King; "you mean that Abul has just been to say that his wife is dead."

"No," replied the Queen, "Abul is dead."

"Not at all," returned the King; "Abul's wife is dead," and they fell out and quarrelled about it.

Then the King said: "Well, we'll make a contract: if I am wrong, then I'll give you a present of a garden."

And the Queen said: "Very well; and if I am mistaken, I will give you my picture gallery."

On this the King and Queen together went with a number of followers to the house of Abul.

When Abul and his wife saw them coming they were so frightened that they did not know what to do, and, having no time to run away, they both got under the cloth they were sewing, and lay quite still as though they were dead.

The King and Queen coming up were surprised indeed to find that both were really dead; but the King, remembering his promise to his wife, said: "Now, if we only could find out who died first."

On this Abul crept out quietly, fell at the King's feet, and cried: "Your Majesty, I died first."

At the same time his wife crawled out and prostrated herself at the Queen's feet, saying: "Your Majesty, I died first."

All the followers began to laugh, and so did the King, who asked Abul why he had done this thing. Abul then confessed how he had squandered all the money which the King had given, and, not knowing how to get any more, had determined to do what he had done.

The King, pleased at Abul's cleverness, gave him houses and money, so that he never again suffered any want.

THE MAGICIAN AND THE MERCHANT

ONE day a merchant, going for a stroll, came across a date tree; reaching up his hand, he plucked a date and threw the stone away.

Now, near the spot where it fell there lived a wicked magician, who suddenly appeared before the frightened merchant, and told him he was going to kill him.

"You have put out my son's eye," said he, "by throwing the stone into it, and now you shall pay for the deed with your life."

The poor merchant begged and implored for mercy, but the magician refused. At last the merchant asked that he might be allowed to go home and settle his affairs, and distribute his goods amongst his family, after which he promised to return.

To this the magician consented, so the merchant departed, and spent a last happy year with his wife and children. Then, after dividing his goods amongst them, bade them farewell, and with many tears, left them, that he might return to the magician and fulfil his promise.

Arrived at the spot, he saw an old man, who asked him why he came to such a place. "A wicked magician lives here," said he, "who kills people, or else changes them into animals or birds."

"Alas!" cried the unfortunate merchant, "that is just what my fate will be, for I have come in fulfilment of a promise to return after a year and be killed."

Just then two other old men came, and, while the four were conversing together, the magician, sword in hand, suddenly appeared and rushed at the merchant to kill him.

On this the old man interceded, and said: "O Magician, if what I have suffered be more than you have suffered in the loss of your son's eye, then indeed give this man double punishment: let me, I beg you, tell my story."

"Say on," said the magician.

"Do you see this deer?" said the old man; "it is my wife. I was once married to a wife, but after a time I wearied of her, and married another wife, who presented me with a son. I took both the woman and her child to my first wife, and asked her to feed and take care of them; but she, being jealous, changed my wife into a cow, and my son into a calf. After a year I returned and enquired after my wife and child. My first wife said: 'Your wife is dead, and for the last two days your child has been missing.'

"Now it happened at that time that I wanted to offer a sacrifice, and, asking for a suitable offering, my second wife was brought to me. She fell at my feet, and looked so unhappy that I could not kill her, and sent her away. Then my wife grew very angry, and insisted upon the sacrifice. At last I consented, and the poor cow was killed.[1]

"Then I asked for another offering, and the calf was brought. It too looked at me with tearful eyes, and I had not the heart to kill it, but gave it to a cowherd, and told him to bring it back to me after a year. He kept it with his other cattle, and one day a young girl who saw it began to

[1] This story was told by a Mahamedan woman, and I should think it was of Mahamedan origin, as no Hindu would even distantly refer to the slaughter of a cow, and such a story told by a Mahamedan to a Hindu would cause intense ill-feeling.

laugh and cry. On this the cowherd asked her reason for such conduct, and she replied: 'That calf is not really what it appears to be, but is a young man, and his mother was the cow who was sacrificed some time ago.'

"Then the cowherd ran to me and told me the girl's story, and I went at once to her to ask whether it was really true, and if she could not restore my son to his original shape again. 'Yes,' she replied, 'on two conditions. One, that I may be allowed to marry your son, and the other, that I may do as I please with your first wife.'

"To this I consented, so she took some water and sprinkled it upon the calf, which at once turned into my son again. With some of the same water she sprinkled my wife, who there and then turned into a deer.

"Now, I might easily kill her if I liked; but, knowing that she is my wife, I take her with me wherever I go."

Then the second old man said: "Hear my story. I was one of three brothers. My father died, and we divided his clothes and money amongst us. My eldest brother and I became merchants, but my third brother ran away, wasted and squandered his money, and became a beggar. He returned home, and begged us to forgive him, which we did, and gave him one thousand rupees to buy merchandise.

"We three then went across the seas to buy goods. On the seashore I saw a very beautiful woman, and asked her if she would come across the sea with me. She consented; but when my brothers saw her they grew jealous, and, as soon as the ship sailed, they took her and threw her into the sea, and me after her. But she, being an Enchanted Being, rose to the surface of the water unhurt, and, taking me up, carried me to a place of safety on the seashore.

"Then she said she was very angry with my brothers and meant to kill them both. I begged in vain that she would spare them, so at last she consented to punish them in some other way instead of killing them.

"When next I visited at the house of my brothers, two dogs fell at my feet and cowered before me. Then the woman told me that they were my brothers, and would remain dogs for twelve years, after which time they would resume their natural shapes."

The third old man began to tell his story. "I had the misfortune to marry a witch, who, soon after my marriage, turned me into a dog. I fled from the house, and ate such scraps of food as were thrown away by the store-keepers in the market place.

"One day one of the men there took me home, but his daughter turned away her head each time she looked at me. At last her father enquired her reason for doing this, and she replied: 'Father, that is not a dog, but a man whose wife is a witch, and it is she who has changed him into a dog. I will restore him again to his former shape.' So she sprinkled water upon me, and I forthwith regained the shape of a man. I then asked her if I might not punish my wife, and she gave me some water and told me to go and sprinkle it upon the wicked witch.

"I did this, and she became a donkey! Yet I keep her, and take care of her, and pray you, even as we had mercy, to so have mercy upon this man."

So the magician forgave the man, and let him go.

THE SNAKE AND THE FROG

A Rajah had two sons. The eldest ascended the throne after his father's death, but fearing lest his brother might interfere with him, he ordered him to be killed.

The poor boy, hearing of this order, quietly left the house and escaped into the jungles, where he saw a snake with a frog in its mouth which it was trying to swallow.

As the young Rajah approached, he heard the frog say: "Oh, if God would only send some one to rescue me from the snake, how thankful I should be."

The Rajah, full of pity, threw a stone at the snake, and it immediately released the frog, which hopped away.

The snake remained still, dazed by the hurt received by the stone. Now, the Rajah felt sorry for it, and thought to himself: "I have taken away its natural food;" so, quickly cutting off a piece of his own flesh, he threw it to the snake, saying: "Here, take this instead."

The snake took it home, and when its wife saw it, she said: "This is very good flesh; where did you get it?"

The snake told her what had happened, and she said: "Go back to that man and reward him for what he has done."

Then the snake assumed the form of a man, and, going back to the Rajah, said: "I will be your servant, if you will take me."

The Rajah agreed, and his new servant followed him.

The frog, meantime, had also gone home and told his wife of the narrow escape he had from the snake, and how a man had saved him from its very jaws.

"Go back," said she, "and serve him, to prove your gratitude."

So he also took the form of a man and offered himself as a servant to the Rajah. "Come," said he, "and we three will live together."

Then they entered a city belonging to a great King, and the three of them offered to work for him.

"But," said the young Rajah, "I will

only work on condition that you pay me a thousand rupees a day."

To this the King agreed, and they were employed by him.

The young Rajah gave his own two followers one hundred rupees a day; and, after putting aside one hundred for his own requirements, distributed the rest in charity.

One day the King went to take a bath in the tank, or pond, and while bathing, his ring slipped off and fell into the water.

He therefore called the young Rajah and said to him: "Go and get my ring which is in that tank."

This made the youth very sad, "For," thought he, "how am I to get a ring from the bottom of a tank?"

But his servant who had once been a frog begged him not to be sad, and said: "I will get it for you."

So, quickly taking his old form, he dived into the water and restored the ring to his master, who took it to the King.

Some time after this the King's daughter was bitten by a snake, and in great danger of death. "Make my child well," demanded the King of the young Rajah. But this was hard to do, and the youth became sadder than ever.

"Do not despair," said his servant who had once been a snake, "but put me into the room where the child is, for I understand the treatment for snake-bite."

As soon as this was done he sucked out all the poison, and the child rccovered.

This so delighted the King that he called the young Rajah and offered him his daughter in marriage as a reward.

So the marriage took place, and they lived happily ever afterwards.

THE BARBER AND THE THIEF

A THIEF entered the house of a barber, and, carefully making bundles of all he could lay hands upon, was about to take them away when the barber spied him; and, quickly getting out of bed, sat down at the door, thus cutting off the way of escape for the thief, who waited in vain for him to move.

The barber sat smoking his *hookah*,[1] and every now and then refreshed himself by drinking water, occasionally spitting at what looked like a bundle of rags on the floor; but which was in reality the thief.[2] After a while the barber woke his wife by flinging a little water on her. She woke up very angry, and scolded him roundly.

"What!" said the barber, "you mind a

[1] An Indian pipe.

[2] To spit upon a man in the East is considered the greatest of dignities.

little water being thrown at you, while this man"—pointing to the thief—"has no objection to being spat upon!"

Then the thief found he had been discovered, and implored forgiveness.

Thinking he had already suffered sufficient indignities, they forgave him and let him go.

THE STORY OF PURAN

THERE was once a shoemaker who had a vegetable garden in which grew a bed of brinjals (or egg plant). Unknown to him, a fairy used sometimes to come and walk there; and one day, while passing the brinjal bushes, a thorn on them caught one of her wings and broke it, so that she was unable to fly, and had to remain where she was.

Next time the shoemaker visited his garden he saw a beautiful woman in it; and, not knowing that she was a fairy, asked her to tell him her name, and how she came there.

Her only reply was: "I am cold: give me a covering, I pray you."

Then he invited her to take shelter in his hut, and gave her a *lowie,* or warm covering, saying: "Take this and stay as long as you like, and be my daughter."

The shoemaker had a kind heart, and was very good to his adopted child, whom he named "Loonar Chumari."

Now a Rajah, by name Suliman, sometimes visited the shoemaker's shop; and when he saw the fairy he fell in love with her, and begged for her hand in marriage.

The shoemaker consented, and after a time the marriage took place; but Suliman had another wife at his Palace, and a son whose name was Puran: and he was most anxious to find out whether, when he grew up, this son would make a good ruler, so he sent for a Brahmin and enquired.

"Yes," declared the Brahmin, "he will be a good ruler, but you must keep him locked up for twelve years in an underground room."

This was done, and at the time when Suliman met the fairy, the twelve years had nearly been completed; but the boy refused to remain even a week longer, for he was weary of being locked up for so long. Even his own mother could not influence him in the matter, and so he was released.

Now Puran was a very comely youth,

and when he made his obeisance to his new stepmother, she was greatly impressed with his handsome face, and thought to herself: "Had I not been in such a hurry I might have married him instead of Suliman."

The thought vexed her so much that she made up her mind to get Puran out of her sight by having him killed. She told Suliman that his boy was wanting in respect towards her, and deserving of death.

On hearing this, Suliman had a bowl of boiling oil prepared, and, calling his son, said: "My son, if this be indeed true about you, plunge your hand into this boiling oil: if you are innocent no harm will come to you."

Puran, without a sign of fear, did as his father bid him, and plunged in his hand, taking it out without a mark.

Then Suliman turned to his wife and said: "See, the oil does not burn him."

But she replied angrily: "Never mind, I am not content, and shall not rest day or night until you have his eyes put out, and both his hands and his feet cut off, after which you must have him flung into a pit."

Suliman, who was completely under the power of the fairy, at last consented to this, and gave the order; but Puran's own mother pleaded so earnestly that her boy's eyes might be spared, that the servants felt sorry for her; and, substituting the eyes of an animal, they left the young man's eyes untouched.

Then Puran was thrown into a pit and there left.

A Guru, or Priest, who lived near that place used to send his followers daily to bring food and water for him, and one of them, mistaking the dry pit for a well, let down his *chattie* for water. Whereupon Puran, whose hands and feet had been restored by the Almighty, caught hold of the *chattie* and would not let it go.

The Guru called out: "Let go, or I will bring my book of incantations and crush you into dust."

"Try," replied a voice from the bottom of the pit, "for I too can bring my books and crush you to dust."

The Guru was frightened, and, returning to the head Guru, his master, told him what had happened.

Then the old Guru said: "It must be Puran; I will go and see." So, taking with him a ball of raw cotton, he called out at the top of the pit: "Puran, is that you? If so, and you are an innocent man, I will let down a thread of raw cotton, and you will be able to climb up by it, for it will not break if used by the innocent."

"Let it down," replied Puran, and he climbed up safely.

The Guru looked at him as he stood up, and then quietly returned to his own home.

There he met all his pupils or followers, who are called "Cheelas," and sent them out to bring stores. There were one hundred and thirty-five Cheelas, and before they left he warned them, saying: "Go everywhere except to that magic country where those women live who practise witchcraft."

But the men were curious, and, in spite of the warning, went to the witches' country.

The witches saw them coming, and laughed gleefully. "Let us play a trick on these young Gurus," they said, "and turn them all into young bulls."

This they did, and, leading the creatures

to their husbands, said: "See what fine bulls we have brought in exchange for two and a half pounds of flour."

The husbands were very pleased, and kept the bulls to carry loads.

Meanwhile the old Guru waited for his followers, but as none of them appeared, he sought the aid of his books and discovered what had happened.

Then he pronounced his incantations and dried up all the water in the country, with the exception of one well, near which he sat.

The witches soon found that they would die of thirst, so they came to the old man's well, but they barely had time to put down their *chatties* before he turned the lot of them into donkeys and let them graze.

Very soon the witches were missed by their husbands, who came to the old Guru and asked if he could give any news.

"How can I tell," said he, "when one hundred and thirty-five of my own Gurus are lost and I cannot find them."

"But you can recall them, our Father," said the men.

"That is what I mean to do;" and so saying, the Guru took out his books and began to read. While he did this, they saw in the distance a herd of one hundred and thirty-five bulls approaching, and each one carried a load of wood or hay.

They stood still before the old Guru, who then restored them to their former shapes.

Then the witches' husbands were amazed, and said: "O Guru! can you not call our wives also?"

"Call them yourselves, my friends, as you have seen me call my men."

But the men knew nothing of either witchcraft or incantations, so they besought the Guru to help them.

At last he agreed, and asked for a thick, strong stick, which he gave into the hands of one of his Cheelas, and said: "Go knock each of those donkeys a blow on the head with this."

The Cheela did as he was told, and the donkeys resumed the shapes of women, all but five old ones which the Guru said must remain donkeys by way of warning.

Then the Guru sent his followers forth as before, and coming to the pit where Puran had been found, they saw a dry stick standing near it. "This will do for fire," said they;

but when they touched it a feeble voice was heard.

So they reported the matter to thc old Guru, and when he touched the stick it said, "Guru Jee." On this he recognised Puran, who for years had waited beside the well.

"Why did you not go home, my son?"

"Because you did not tell me," said Puran, "so I waited here for your orders."

Then the Guru held him tenderly and washed the mud off him, and in many days he grew strong again.

"Now go home to your parents," said the Guru.

But Puran said: "No, I will remain with you."

Thus in time he became a very highly respected Guru.

TABARISTAN

In the country called Tabaristan there lived a rich Rajah, who gave a feast and invited a number of guests.

Amongst the guests came a stranger who partook of the good things distributed. The Rajah, on seeing him, enquired who he was.

"I am a stranger," said he, "but am willing to serve you, as I have come from a very distant country."

The Rajah said he would keep him as a sort of *Chowkidar*, to guard his house at night. So all night long the stranger used to pace up and down the Palace grounds keeping watch.

One night the Rajah came out and, seeing him pacing up and down, asked him who he was.

"Why, I am he whom you engaged as a servant."

Hardly had he spoken when a loud cry

echoed through the grounds, and a voice said: "I am going on, I am going on!"

"What is that?" asked the Rajah.

"I do not know," said the man, "but I hear it every night."

"Go and find out," returned the Rajah. So the man turned to do his bidding.

Now the Rajah was very curious, and, quickly wrapping himself in his coat, quietly followed his servant.

Outside the garden gate sat a figure covered and clothed in loose white garments.

On approaching it the servant said: "Who are you?"

"I am Time," replied the figure, "and hold the Rajah's life, which is now nearly over."

"Cannot anything be done to spare it?" asked the man.

"Yes, it can be spared by the sacrifice of another, and that one must be your son."

"I will give not only my son's life, but the lives of all my family and my own," replied the man; "but, if you want only my son, you may have him."

Then he went and told his son, who said: "Gladly will I give my life, for what is it in comparison with the life of a Rajah? Come, father, take me soon that I may die."

Then the man led his son to the veiled figure, and said: "Here is my son; he is willing to die."

Taking a knife, he was about to plunge it into his child when the figure cried: "Enough! You have proved that you were willing not only to give your son, but your whole family, and the Almighty is pleased to spare the Rajah's life for another seven years."

Now the Rajah, who had heard every word of the interview, quickly returned to the spot where he had first heard the voice, and there awaited his servant's return.

"Well, what was the sound?" asked he, when he saw him.

"A man and a woman had quarrelled," replied the servant, "but I have managed to reconcile them, and they have promised not to quarrel for seven years."

Then the Rajah left him, and ordered him to appear at his Court the following day.

Next day, when the Court was full, the Rajah addressed all his people, and said: "I am resolved to give up my throne and all I possess to this man; for last night, unknown to me, he was willing to give up, not only his son's life but his own, and the lives of all his family, in order to save mine, and for my sake."

The poor servant was deeply touched and astonished at the turn matters had so unexpectedly taken, but the Rajah was firm in his resolve, and left his throne and his kingdom.

The servant then became Rajah, and ruled wisely and well to the end of his days.

THE PAINTED JACKAL

A JACKAL had the habit of visiting the kitchens of several people at night and eating whatever it could find.

One day, in visiting the house of a dyer, it put its head into a deep vessel containing blue dye, and, finding the mixture was not good to eat, tried to get its head out again, but could not do so for some time. When at last it managed to escape, its head was dyed a beautiful dark blue colour.

He ran away into the jungles, glad to escape, and unconscious of his strange appearance; but the other animals in the jungle thought some new animal had come, and were quite charmed, so that they created him their King.

They divided up all the wild creatures, and put their new King next to the jackals, so that when they cried out at nights, he cried too, and nobody found out that he was only a jackal.

But one day some young jackals made him angry, so he turned them out and ordered the wolves and foxes to remain nearest to him.

That night, when he began to cry and howl, it was at once discovered that he was only a jackal; so all the animals ran at him, bit him, and turned him out.

THE ENCHANTED BIRD, MUSIC, AND STREAM

THERE was once a Prince who used to amuse himself by dressing as a poor man, and going about amongst his subjects without their finding out who he was.

In this way he found out all that they did, and how they lived.

Once, while walking through a gully, he saw three sisters, and overheard their conversation.

One said: "If I could marry even a servant of the Prince, how happy I should be! I should eat sweets and all sorts of nice things all day long."

The other sister said: "I'd rather marry his cook, for then I should get still better things."

But the third sister said: "I'd like best to marry the Prince himself, for then I'd get the best things of all to eat."

The Prince went home, and next day, while holding court, gave an order that these three sisters should be brought to him.

The order was immediately carried out, and, as the three trembling girls stood before him, they wondered much why they had been summoned.

"Now," said he, "tell me what you three were talking about last night?"

Terribly alarmed, the eldest confessed that she had said she would like to be the wife of one of the servants, so as to get nice things to eat. The second said she had wished to be the wife of his cook.

The third sister hesitated, and then said timidly that she had dared to say she would like best to be the wife of the Prince himself.

On this the Prince said: "You may have your wishes."

He then ordered the one to be married to one of his servants, and the other to his cook; but the third he married himself.

Some time after this, a son was born; but his wife's two sisters, who had begged to be present upon the occasion, and who were very jealous of their sister's position, quietly removed the baby, and put a dog's puppy in its place. The baby they put into a box and flung into the river.

Now the Prince's gardener found the box and opened it; and, when he saw what it contained, he was overjoyed, and took the child to his wife, telling her that God had at last given her a son which he would keep and bring up as his own son.

Meantime, the Prince was very angry indeed, but forgave his wife at the request of her friends.

Some time after this another son was born, which the sisters changed for a kitten, and, putting the babe into a box, threw it into the river as before; but again the gardener found the child and carried him to his wife.

Yet a third child was born to the Princess, a little girl, which the two sisters changed for a rat. As before, they placed the child in a box and threw it into the river; and yet a third time did the gardener rescue the babe, and take it to grow up with its two brothers, his adopted boys.

By this time the Prince was very angry with his wife, and turned her out of his house.

The gardener and his wife, who had loved their adopted children very dearly, died when the boys were about eight or nine years of age.

So the boys begged the Prince to give them land of their own, on which to build or cultivate; and he, remembering how fond his gardener had always been of them, granted their request, so they lived there very happily with their little sister.

The brothers often went out hunting, and on one occasion, when they were out and their sister alone at home, a very old woman came to her and begged for some water. She willingly gave it, and then asked the old woman very kindly if she would not come in and rest. "Come and see my house," she said, "and tell me what you think of it."

The old woman said: "You have everything very nice, but there are three things which you have not got."

"And what are those?"

"You have no bird, no music, and no stream of water," replied the old woman; "without these your house is nothing."

"Where am I to get them?"

"You must go to the West."

So saying, she went away and left the girl very sad, for she wished for the three things without which her home was incomplete.

On the return of her brothers, they asked her why she looked so sad; and she told them of the old woman's visit, and what she had said.

"If that is all," cried the eldest brother, "I will go and bring you all three things."

The sister at first cried very much, and begged of him not to go, but at last she consented; and as he bade her good-bye, he gave her a string of beads, saying: "As long as I am well, these beads will be separate from each other; but should any misfortune overtake me, or I should die, the beads will be no longer separate, but will be joined together."

Then he mounted his horse and rode away.

On the way he met an old Fakir. This old man's face was covered with hair, so that he could not see, and he had a very long grey beard.

The boy looked at him, and said: "Let me shave you, and you will be able to see better."

So the Fakir allowed himself to be shaved,

after which he asked the youth where he was going, and on hearing, he advised him not to go. "For," said he, "many have already gone on that quest, but have never returned."

Yet the boy persisted. So the old Fakir gave him a ball, and said: "Keep throwing this before you as you go. Stop where the ball stops, and heed no sounds or interruptions on the way."

The ball went in the direction ot a high mountain, and the boy followed; but in the mountain there were strange hissing sounds and voices all around, which kept shouting to him, and asking who he was and where he came from.

He paid no heed to these, until suddenly there came a great clap of thunder, followed by an earthquake. This so startled the boy that he looked round, and in a moment was turned into stone.

The poor little sister at home, discovering that she could no longer separate her beads, was grieved indeed, knowing that some harm had befallen her brother; and she wept bitterly.

On this her second brother said he would

go and seek him, and also find the three things she required for her house.

His sister implored him not to leave her, for he was all she had left; but he was determined, so she was obliged to reluctantly consent to his going.

Before leaving he gave her a flower, and said: "Sister, as long as this flower keeps fresh, you will know that I am alive and well; but if it should close or fade, you may feel sure that I too am dead."

Then he mounted his steed and started on his journey.

Soon he met the old Fakir, who warned him as he had warned his brother, saying: "My son, so many have gone on this quest and have lost their lives; your own brother has lost his life, and yet you wish to go. Turn back, I advise you."

"No," said the boy, "I am determined to find my brother, and also the bird, music, and stream of water."

Then the Fakir gave him also a ball of string, with the same directions which he had given his brother; and he continued on his journey.

As he reached the hill, he too heard the

same hissing, shouting, and cries to stop; but he heeded nothing, until at last came the peal of thunder and earthquake, which so terrified him that he turned round to look, and he too was turned into stone.

At home his poor sister saw her flower fade away and die, and then she knew that her other brother had also come to an untimely end.

So she arose and locked her door, and said: "I will go myself and find my brothers."

On her way she met the same old Fakir, who accosted her, and asked her whither she was going.

He was much grieved when she told him her story, and said: "Brave men have lost their lives, and you, a woman, without half their strength, are going. I pray you be advised and return."

"No, no," she returned; "if *men* have lost their courage, I, a *woman*, shall not lose mine. I am very brave, and I mean to go."

So the Fakir bade her God-speed very sadly, and gave her the same parting gift as he had given her brothers, directing her what to do with it.

The first thing she did was to buy some

cotton wool, and with it stop her ears, so that she could not hear a sound; then she proceeded on her journey up the hill.

The same sounds followed her all the way, but she heard them not, nor did she hear the thunder or heed the earthquake in her anxiety to find her brothers.

On and on went she, until she saw a cage hanging on a tree, and in it a bird. She took it with great joy, and said: "I have found my bird, and have only the music and water to get for my home to be perfect."

To her delight, the bird heard, and replied: "If you break off a branch of that tree and stick it into the ground, the breeze through its leaves will make the sweetest music you have ever heard; and if you will take a little water from that enchanted stream yonder, and pour it into your garden, it will never cease to flow. Thus you will have both music and stream."

The girl did as the bird advised, and heard the sweetest melody in the branch of the tree. Then she filled a vessel with water and prepared to return, but very sorrowfully, for she had found both her brothers turned into stone.

She told her trouble to the bird, who said: "Sprinkle some of the water on the stones."

This she did, and, to her great surprise, both the lads came to life.

They were delighted to see her, and to know that she had succeeded in finding the gifts they had failed to get; and the three returned home and lived very happily together for some time.

One day the two brothers thought they would like to go out hunting again.

Now they did not know that an order had been passed that nobody was to hunt in that forest except the Prince, and, while they were there, they came face to face with the Prince himself. This alarmed them, and they tried to hide themselves; but he called them, and enquired why they were hunting there against orders.

Then they explained that they were in ignorance of his orders when they came, and begged forgiveness.

The Prince, pleased at their appearance, enquired who they were, and they said: "The adopted sons of your gardener who died some time ago. Our own parents died when we were young."

Then the Prince invited them to his Palace, but they said they could go nowhere without first telling their sister.

"Well, ask your sister," said he, "and come to-morrow."

On the third day they met the Prince again, and he asked why they had not come; but they pleaded as an excuse that they had forgotten to ask their sister. The Prince then gave them a golden ball and said: "When you see this, you will remember."

That night as they were going to bed, the small golden ball rolled out on the floor, and seeing it, they remembered, and told their sister of the Prince's invitation.

She was very displeased with them for not having complied with it earlier; and told them that they must go and see him the very next day.

On the morrow the two boys went to the Palace, where the Prince received them very kindly, and gave them all sorts of good things to eat and drink, saying to himself: "Had I had children, they would by this time be the same ages as these lads."

One day, soon after this, the bird advised

the sister of the boys to invite the Prince to dinner.

"How can I entertain so grand a man?" said she.

"Make him a dish of *kheer* (rice cooked with milk and sugar); and besides this, to please him, another dish of pearls."

"But where shall I get the pearls?"

"Send a man to dig beneath that tree, and you will find as many as you require," replied the bird.

So the girl did as she was told, and sent a man to dig. He soon found a box full of pearls, and these she placed in a very beautiful dish, and put it alongside the plate of *kheer*.

The Prince accepted the invitation to dinner, and came to the house.

After showing him all round, the girl led him at last to the room in which she had prepared dinner; and as her bird was also there, she told it to make a *salaam* to the Prince, which it did.

Then the first dish was uncovered, and the Prince knew that he could not eat it as it was made of pearls; but the bird spoke up and said: "O Prince! are you not yet able to understand the difference between pearls and dross? When your wife bore your children, you believed them to be dogs, cats, or rats, and turned out your poor wife, who was in reality the mother of these"—and she pointed to the two boys and their sister—"your own children, who were exchanged by their wicked aunts for a dog, a cat, a rat, and you believed them."

On hearing this, the Prince was astounded; and then the bird told him exactly all that had taken place.

Delighted to be once more united to his children, he sought his poor wife, and, throwing himself at her feet, besought her with tears to forgive him.

This she very gladly did, and returned with him to the Palace, where her children received her; and they were all very happy ever after.

The two wicked sisters were killed by order of the Prince.

THE DOG TEMPLE

About eleven miles from Raipur, near the village of Jagasar, is a temple built to the memory of a faithful dog of the Bunjara species, and this is the story of how it came to be built.

Many years ago a Bunjara Naik, or headman of the clan of Bunjaras, or wandering traders, owed money to a "Marwari," or money-lender at Raipur.

When pressed for payment, the Bunjara, who was then standing near the Marwari's shop, said: "Here is my gold necklace, and here is my faithful dog: keep both till I return to my camping-ground near Jagasar, and fetch you the money."

The necklace and dog were then left as security, and the man went his way.

That night the Marwari's shop was broken into by thieves, and many valuables stolen, among them the golden necklace; but, before the thieves could get clear away with their stolen property, the dog got up and barked and leaped about, and made so much noise that the Marwari and his men got up, caught the thieves, and recovered the property, which was of considerable worth.

The Marwari was very pleased, and out of gratitude for what the dog had done, determined to cancel and forgive the debt of his master, the Bunjara. So he wrote a paper to cancel it, tied it to the dog's neck and let it go, saying: "Carry the tidings to your owner."

Early next morning the dog trotted off, and was nearing the camping-ground which was his home, when the Bunjara saw him, and, very displeased, he took a stick and struck the poor dog across the head, saying: "You brute! you could not remain even twenty-four hours with the Marwari, though my honour was at stake."

The blow killed the dog on the spot, and as he fell, the Bunjara noticed the slip of paper round his neck, and, on reading it, found what joyful news his dog had brought to him. Not only was the debt forgiven, but the reason for it was also stated on the paper.

The grief of the Bunjara was great, for in spite of his hasty temper he loved his dog, as all Bunjaras do. He repented his hasty act, and wept most bitterly over his favourite, vowing that he would try and expiate the deed by building a temple to the faithful dog's memory with the money he had recovered.

The small temple now standing on the spot where this took place testifies to the fulfilment of that vow, and a small dog carved in stone indicates why the Dog Temple was built.

To this day it is deeply revered by all the villagers around, and the story of that faithful dog is often repeated to show how intelligent and true a dog can be.

THE BEAUTIFUL MILKMAID

AT a place called Drug, near Raipur in the Central Provinces of India, there once lived an old woman who had a very beautiful daughter.

The old woman was most unwilling that her daughter should go out into the streets, for she said: "You are so beautiful, my daughter, that I tremble lest any one take you from me."

But the girl replied: "Mother, I must go and earn our daily food. Let me, I pray you, sell milk and curds as usual: no harm will come to me."

The mother very reluctantly let her go; but that day a Rajah happened to pass by and saw her. He noticed how beautiful she was, and stopped his elephant to ask who she was. She told him that she was of humble origin, and only a seller of milk and curds.

"Then," said the Rajah, "I shall buy all that you have."

"Nay," replied the girl; "surely what is mine is yours, and I offer everything in homage to you."

When she persisted in refusing payment the Rajah was angry, and ordered his attendants to scatter the curds, and put the girl into prison for daring to go against his wishes.

The order was obeyed, and the beautiful milkmaid found herself a prisoner.

While in prison she prayed to her Gods for deliverance, and fashioning a parrot out of clay, breathed life into it and told it to go quickly to her lover, a young man grazing his herds in the hills, and tell him what had happened.

The bird flew off and did as he was told; and the lover came down that night with all his clansmen, attacked the Rajah and killed him.

Then he rescued the girl, who lived happily ever after as the wife of her brave deliverer.

A REMEDY FOR SNAKE-BITE

There is in India a small state called Raghoghur, the Rajahs of which are said to possess the power of curing snake-bite, even though it be from the most deadly cobra or karait. This power has been handed down for centuries, and was firmly believed in during the year 1896, and even up to the present moment.

Every man bitten by a deadly snake in that place takes a bit of string, ties seven knots in it, and places it round his neck. As he goes along towards the Palace of the Rajah or Raghoghur, he keeps repeating "Jeth Singh," "Jeth Singh," "Jeth Singh," untying each knot while so doing.

Arrived at the Palace, he salutes the assembled courtiers, and in their presence undoes the last of the seven knots. This done, the Rajah pours water on the bite and on the man's hands. A Brahmin gives his blessing, and he returns to the village cured.

This power descends from father to son, and many are the wonderful cures reported from Raghoghur.

A LEGEND OF SARDANA

In a city called Sardana there once lived a man whose name was Simru. This man had great riches and lands, and also owned a place of worship.

He married a lady of Sardana, who was called "Begum."

After a few years of married life Simru died, and his wealthy widow gave alms and much money to the poor.

In the same city lived an oil dealer who also died, and the angels took him to Heaven and presented him before the Almighty.

"Who have you brought?" asked the Creator. "This man's days upon earth are not yet completed: take him back before his body is buried, and let his spirit re-possess his body; but in the city of Sardana you will find another man of the same name: bring him to me."

On leaving the Court of God, some former

creditor of the oil dealer's, who had preceded him into the Unseen, recognised him, and laying hold of him, demanded the sum of five rupees which he had owed him during his lifetime.

The poor man being unable to pay this debt, the angels once more took him before the Almighty, who asked why they had returned.

The angels replied: "O God, there is a man here to whom this oil dealer owes five rupees, and he will not let us return until the debt is paid."

The Almighty enquired if this was true, and the oil dealer replied: "Yes, but I am a poor man, and not able to repay it."

Then the Almighty said: "In the city of Sardana lives a rich Begum; do you know her?"

"Yes, O King."

"Well, the Begum's treasury is here, and I will advance you five rupees out of it, if, when you return to earth, you promise faithfully to give it back to the Begum."

So the oil dealer gratefully took the loan, paid his debt, and returned with the angels to earth, where he arrived just too late to re-enter his body, which his friends had already taken away to prepare for burial. Watching his opportunity, he waited till they were otherwise engaged, and at once re-entered it; but when he sat up, and began to speak, his terrified friends and relations fled, thinking it was his ghost.

On this the oil dealer called out: "Do not fear, I am not a spirit; but God has released me, as my days upon earth are not yet fulfilled. The man who ought to have died is Kungra, the vegetable man; go and see whether he is dead or alive."

The friends, on going to the house of Kungra, found that he had just fallen from a wall and been killed on the spot; all his relations were wailing and lamenting his sudden end.

Thus everybody knew that the words of the old oil dealer were correct.

In the meantime, the oil dealer called his son, and said: "Son, when I went to Heaven I there met a man to whom I owed five rupees, and he caught me and would not let me return before I paid it, so the Almighty advanced me the money from the Begum's treasury in Heaven, and bade me give her back that amount on my return to earth. Therefore do I entreat you, my son, to come with me, and together we will visit the Begum, and give her five rupees."

So they took the money and went to the Begum's house.

"Who are you?" asked she.

The oil dealer then told her the whole story, ending with: "And now I come to return you the five rupees."

The Begum was very pleased, and, taking the money, she called her servants and ordered a further sum of one hundred rupees to be added to it. This money she spent on sweets, which were distributed amongst the poor.

Many years afterwards the good Begum of Sardana died, but her houses and lands are still in existence; nor does anybody living in that town forget the story of the oilman who died and lived again.[1]

[1] The Begum's property is now in possession of the Jesuits, and the priest who lives there is greatly beloved of the people.

THE STORY OF "BUNJARA TULLAO"

THERE is at a place in India called Agar, a tank or pond known as the "Bunjara Tullao," yet no Bunjara will ever drink water there.

Many years ago no pond existed in that spot, and in all the country round a water famine prevailed, and the poor were perishing for want of water.

A Fakir prophesied that if a man would kill his son and daughter as a sacrifice to the Gods, water would be found and last always.

That night a Bunjara slew his two children, and threw them into a deep hole.

In the morning when the sun shone and people woke up, lo! there was a large pond in place of the hole, and nothing was seen of the unfortunate children. Then the poor filled their *chatties*, and went away rejoicing.

It is said that sometimes the heads of a boy and girl were seen lifted out of the water, and that they held out their hands to passers-by; but because the peasants put mud into them, they discontinued the practice.

In the centre of the "Bunjara Tullao" is a shrine built in memory of its origin.

There is another such pond near the Sipri Bazaar, which remains clear and beautiful, notwithstanding the fact that hundreds of people bathe and wash in it.

The old "Guru" who lives there explains the reason for this.

"Many years ago one of the Gods selected the Sipri Bazaar tank for his bath, and ever since its waters have remained as clear as crystal."

Moral.—Thus there is a cause for everything in the world.

THE ANAR PARI, OR POMEGRANATE FAIRY

Once upon a time there was a King who had seven sons, all of whom were married but the youngest.

One day the Queen-mother spoke to her youngest son, and said: "Why are you not married? Do not the maidens of my Court please thee? Perhaps you want what you cannot get, and that is perfection, unless, indeed, you go and seek and marry the Anar Pari, who is the fairest of all fairies, and whose charms are traditional."

The Prince then and there registered a vow that he would not marry at all unless he found this pearl of great price, and forthwith started on his quest for her.

He put on his armour and five weapons of defence, mounted his favourite steed, and set forth.

He had proceeded a good distance when night fell, and he found himself in a forest near a small hut. Entering it, he found it was occupied by a holy Fakir.

The Fakir said: "My son, why have you come here? Where are you going? And are you not afraid of the wild animals which infest this forest?"

The Prince replied: "Holy Father, I am going on a long journey to try and find the Pomegranate Fairy, so that I may wed her."

"You are going a long way indeed," replied the Fakir; "but if you listen to what I tell you, your journey will not be in vain."

Next morning he called the young man, and told him that he was going to enchant him and turn him into a parrot, so that he might fly to the island on which the fairy was imprisoned, and guarded day and night by seven hundred dreadful dragons. He also told him that on the island he would find a pomegranate tree with three pomegranates on it, of which he was to pluck and bring away the middle one, for in it dwelt the fairy he was so anxious to find.

"But mind you," said the Fakir, "once you have plucked the pomegranate, you are not to wait an instant, or even turn to look back when the dragons come after you, for, if you once look back, all your efforts will be in vain, and you will be killed."

Then the young Prince was turned into a parrot and immediately flew off.

He flew and flew and flew, till he had crossed seven seas; and in the midst of the seventh sea, he at last spied an island in which was a most lovely garden, where grew an exquisite pomegranate tree, and on it three pomegranates, the centre one most beautiful to behold.

He plucked the fruit, and flew as fast as he could, but alas, the dragon who guarded the tree saw him, and called to the other dragons, who, with wild yells and terrifying noises, flew after him.

The young Prince in his flight unfortunately looked back to see where they were, and was immediately burnt to a cinder, and fell to the ground with the golden pomegranate which he had worked so hard to obtain.

The dragons came up and took away the fruit, but left the burnt body of the bird upon the ground.

The Fakir waited long for the return of the parrot, but as it did not come, he set out himself to find it. He was able to cross in safety by making his body invisible, and when he came to the island, the first thing he saw was the burnt body of the parrot lying in the garden.

So he took it up, breathed once more the breath of life into it, and let it go, saying: "Try once more, my son, but remember that I said: '*Look not back*,' but fly to my hut for safety."

Thus saying, he disappeared; and the parrot, watching its chance, very silently approached the tree a second time, stole the fruit, and flew as fast as he could.

The dragons pursued, but he reached the hut in safety; and the old Fakir did not lose a moment, but turned him into a small fly, and then secreted the pomegranate on his person, and sat down.

Almost immediately the dragons also arrived, and said: "Where is the green parrot who stole the fruit?"

"Look and see," said the old Fakir. "I know not what you want; no green parrot is here, nor do I know where the pomegranate is that he took away."

Then he went on quietly counting his beads while the dragons searched everywhere;

but at last, wearied out and finding nothing, they went away, feeling very angry at the loss of their fairy.

As soon as they had gone, the Fakir caused the Prince to resume his original form, and, handing him the pomegranate, said: "Go back to your Palace; and when you have got there, break the pomegranate, and out of it will step the most beautiful woman you have ever seen; take her to be your wife, and may luck go with you."

The young Prince then mounted his steed, and thanked the old Fakir for all his assistance.

As he neared his father's Palace he came to a well in a garden, and having tied his horse to a tree, he went and rested beside the well, and looked at the pomegranate.

"I think I will break it now, and see if a fairy comes out, for if I wait to do so in my father's house before all his courtiers, suppose no fairy appeared, I should be ashamed to death."

So saying, he broke it, and immediately a most lovely woman appeared, bright and dazzling as the sun itself. As soon as he beheld her, he was so entranced that he fell into a swoon. Then the fairy lifted his head very gently, and placing it on her knee, allowed him to sleep on.

While he slept a young woman of low caste came to draw water. Seeing the beautiful fairy, she enquired of her if the sleeping man was the King's youngest son, and if she was the Anar Pari whom he had gone to seek.

Hearing that this was so, she was filled with envy, and planned in her mind how she might take the life of the fairy. So she went up to her, and said: "O fairy, you are most beautiful, but I would be beautiful too if I had on your clothes: come, let us exchange our dresses (or *sarees*), and see how you look in my clothes."

The fairy did as she wished, and the young woman said: "Look how beautiful I am; let us go to the well and behold our reflections in the water to see which is the most beautiful."

The fairy bent forward to see herself, and, as she did so, the young woman pushed her so that she fell into the well and sank into the water.

Having done this, the wicked young woman woke up the Prince, saying: "Come, let us go to the King's Palace."

The Prince looked doubtfully at her, but, being still half asleep, and seeing that she wore the same dress as Anar Pari had on, he assented, believing his passing doubt to be unreasonable.

His arrival at the Palace was made an occasion for great rejoicings, and all were glad that he was at last happily married.

The new Princess would never allow him to leave her, for she feared that he might return to the well; but one day, unknown to her, he found his way there, and looking in, saw floating upon the water a most exquisite lotus lily of pure white, the most perfect flower he had ever seen.

He asked his servants to hook it out for him; but each time they tried to do so, the flower disappeared beneath the water. At last he tried himself to get it, and succeeded easily, for the lily floated towards the hook that he let down.

The Prince took the flower home and looked after it with the greatest care; but when his wife heard where it had come from, she went at night and, tearing it into several pieces, flung it out of the window.

As the broken fragments of the lotus touched the earth, they turned into a bed of mint which grew luxuriantly.

Some of this mint was carried into the King's kitchen, to be used for seasoning dishes; but as the cook began to fry it, a voice was heard from the frying pan, saying: "Here am I, the real Princess, being fried to death, while the wicked woman who threw me into the well has taken my place."

The cook when he heard this was afraid, and threw the mint into the garden again. As soon as it touched the ground it became a lovely creeper, which grew and grew until it gradually approached the bed-chamber of the Prince.

The false Princess when she saw it at once remembered how she had thrown the fragments of the lotus lily into the garden, and, fearing lest this might be an offshoot from it, she ordered her gardener to uproot the creeper and cut it down at once.

The gardener did so, but as he was removing it, the one and only fruit on the tree fell to the ground and rolled under a jessamine bush, where it remained in security.

The gardener's daughter, who came every morning to gather flowers from this bush to weave into garlands, accidentally noticed the fruit lying beneath it, picked it up, and carried it home.

As she entered the gardener's little hut, the fruit fell to the ground and broke open, and out of it stepped the lovely Anar Pari.

The good people of the house were filled with wonder and admiration to see so peerless a being in their humble cottage. They gave her shelter and fed her, the gardener's daughter loving her as a sister, and the gardener as a father.

One day, as the gardener's daughter sat weaving her garlands of jessamine for the King's Court, the fairy said: "Please allow me to make one too; and when it is ready, take it and put it on the neck of the youngest Prince."

So she made it; and when two garlands were completed they were taken to the Prince and Princess. The Princess noticed that the Prince's garland was made in wonderful fashion, and enquired who had made it. They told her that a very lovely woman living in the gardener's hut had made it, and, suspecting at once that this was Anar Pari come to life again, she thought of some plan by which she could destroy her.

The next day she feigned great illness and a very severe headache, which she declared nothing would cure but the placing of a heart of a young and beautiful girl on her forehead. She therefore begged for the heart of the girl who lived in the gardener's hut, and orders were given for her execution.

The gardener and his daughter wept most bitterly, and the executioners were feign to spare the life of so lovely a woman; yet they were obliged to fulfil their orders, so they led the girl to the place of execution.

Before they killed her she begged that her limbs might be scattered to the four winds, and her two eyes thrown upwards into space.

The executioners did as she desired, and her heart was sent to the wicked Princess.

As soon as Anar Pari's eyes were thrown into the air, they became a pair of love-birds and flew into the forest.

Many days after, the Prince went to hunt in the forest, and was resting himself under the trees when he heard two love-birds talking in the branches, and one was telling the other the story of her life. How she was once Anar Pari, a beautiful fairy, and how a wicked woman had enticed her away from the side of the Prince while he slept, and thrown her down a well, and how the woman was now reigning in her stead as Princess at the Palace.

The young Prince was amazed to hear all this, and looking up, cried: "I have at last found you. Come down and be my Fairy Princess once again."

Then two laughing, loving eyes appeared, and presently they were set in the form of a woman, and the Prince once again beheld the world-renowned form of Anar Pari.

They went together to the Palace, and there the Prince ordered the false Princess to be brought out, and told everybody present the story of her wickedness.

The sentence passed upon her was that she was to be buried alive near the well; this was done, and to this day nobody dare go near it. Then the Prince married the fairy, and they lived happily ever afterwards; but the old gardener and his daughter were not forgotten, and very often the beautiful Princess sat with her friends, and the two girls weaved garlands together, and spoke lovingly of the time when Anar Pari had dwelt in the old hut in the garden.